The Restoration of Organs

Da Capo Press Music Reprint Series

MUSIC EDITOR

BEA FRIEDLAND
Ph.D., City University of New York

The Restoration of Organs

By JOHN MATTHEWS

Da Capo Press • New York • 1982

Library of Congress Cataloging in Publication Data

Matthews, John, 1856-
   The restoration of organs.

   (Da Capo Press music reprint series)
   Reprint. Originally published: 2nd ed. London :
Office of "Musical Opinion", 1920.
   Includes index.
   1. Organ—Maintenance and repair. I. Title.
ML552.M18   1981   786.6'3   81-12541
ISBN 0-306-76098-3   AACR2

This Da Capo Press edition of *The Restoration of Organs* is an unabridged
republication of the second edition published in London in 1920, here
supplemented with a Foreword by Barbara Owen.

Foreword copyright © 1982 by Barbara Owen

Published by Da Capo Press, Inc.
A Subsidiary of Plenum Publishing Corporation
233 Spring Street, New York, N.Y. 10013

Manufactured in the United States of America

FOREWORD

IN RECENT years there has been a renewal of interest in the older organs—most of them dating from the mid- or late-nineteenth century—found in many of the smaller American churches. Credit must be given to organizations such as the Organ Historical Society for fostering the appreciation and encouraging the preservation of these instruments. While not long ago it was fashionable to rebuild, electrify, or otherwise disfigure such organs, today the emphasis is on restoration, and some organ building firms have found it advantageous to specialize in this work. In some instances, however, funds are unavailable for professional restoration, and the work is undertaken by well-meaning amateurs with varying results.

There has long been a need for a guidebook to assist the amateur repairer and restorer of old organs. Curiously, such a work—the present volume—has been in existence since 1920, although long out of print. As its subtitle indicates, it is intended for the "country organist" who may be faced with the need of doing repairs on his own. Matthews, an organist himself, speaks as one having had professional experience working with an organ builder. While the date and place of writing must be borne in mind in certain instances, the information given is in general surprisingly up-to-date, and as applicable to old American organs as to English ones.

Given a well-equipped workshop and experience in woodworking and mechanics, it would indeed be possible to restore an old tracker-action organ of modest proportions solely with the advice found in this book, and organbuilders having no prior experience with this type of organ could in fact benefit from a study of Matthews's procedures. Of more general value, however, will be the author's many practical suggestions for simple repairs and maintenance, provided always that those who attempt such procedures for the first time take to heart Matthews's frequent reminders on the essential fragility of action parts and pipes, and the need to proceed with utmost care and caution.

BARBARA OWEN
Newburyport, Mass.
February, 1981

The Restoration of Organs.

A PRACTICAL GUIDE TO THE ORGANIST
IN COUNTRY AND ISOLATED PARISHES.

The Restoration of

Organs.

By JOHN MATTHEWS.

Author of "A Handbook on the Organ"
(Augener Edition)
and Organist of St. Stephen's Church, Guernsey.

Second Edition.

Price 5s. net.

LONDON: OFFICE OF "MUSICAL OPINION,"
CHICHESTER CHAMBERS, CHANCERY LANE, W.C.2.
1920.

Printed by the Proprietors of *Musical Opinion* (A. W. Fitzsimmons and W. P. Fitzsimmons) at Chichester Chambers, Chancery Lane, London.

The Restoration of Organs.

INTRODUCTION.

A NEW edition of this book having been called for, the author avails himself of the opportunity to amplify various sections, in order to increase its usefulness.

Many excellent articles have appeared in *Musical Opinion* dealing with every branch of piano and reed organ repair, but organ news somehow has been mainly confined to the compiling of fancy specifications. These "castles in the air" are fascinating, no doubt, but not very helpful, since the same paper scheme, executed by a dozen different builders, would result in the most surprising differences in effect and in actual value.

It is believed that these articles— which originally appeared in *Musical Opinion*—revised and presented in book form, will be of service to many who have not hitherto had to examine very closely the dark and dusty interiors of the organs they play. It makes no claim to be a treatise on the art of organ building, but is intended to help those who have good reason to be dissatisfied with various defects in their organs, and who are yet unaware of the real cause and nature of those defects, and who may not be in the happy position of being able to give *carte blanche* to a good builder for a complete rebuild.

An organ is at once the most costly and the least understood feature in the furnishing of a church. In fact, so many and varied are the blunders perpetrated in relation to it, that an expert would have to think hard before citing half-a-dozen ideal cases wherein the architect, the designer, and the builder of the organ, supported by an organ committee and congregation providing ample funds, have all combined to secure the best possible result! In the great majority of instances, one or other of the following brief criticisms would apply. "Badly balanced; pedal organ starved." "A cheap, competitive affair, with much penny-wise-and-pound-foolish economy shown; will soon require extensive repairs." "A good instrument spoilt by a bad position; builder to be pitied for having to arrange it thus against his better judgment." "Originally a good example of its period, but needs judicious rebuilding; parts of it are excellent."

If the organ were considered as a collection of instruments brought into one harmonious whole with more or less skill by the designer, builder and voicer, it would be better realised by the general public that its merits or demerits cannot be so quickly summed up as in the case of any other musical instrument, for it involves so many more trades and art-crafts, a failure in any one vitiating the whole.

And now, to plunge at once into our subject, we will take the case of an organist, vicar and churchwardens anxious to know what may be done to repair the ravages of time in their organ.

If the instrument is by one of the good craftsmen of, let us say, the Victorian period—such as Willis, Lewis, Hill, Robson, Walker, Bishop, Bryceson, Holdich, &c. — there is a strong presumption in favour of its containing a good deal that is worth preserving; side by side with a good deal that needs restoration or replacing in proportion to the years of neglect. Let us begin, as old Bach always did, with a bellows test, "to see if it had good lungs." If hand-blown, the player should be able to hold down the chord of C major on the full organ coupled to the CCC and CC of the full pedal in octaves without any unsteadiness or frantic exertions on the part of the blower. If the tell-tale rises too rapidly on the bellows being filled and no demand made on the wind at the key-board, leakages must be searched for. When serious, they will reveal themselves by black seams along the folds of the ribs, the white leather being affected in this way. These may, of course, be temporarily staunched by glueing strips of thin white leather over them until it is convenient or necessary to have the bellows removed for re-leathering throughout. But hand-blowing is happily becoming a thing of the past wherever electricity, water or gas power can be substituted, and here there enters a great advantage in favour of the modern system of blowing by means of fans: though the bellows area may be lamentably deficient for hand blowing—especially if additions not contemplated by the original builder have been made—it will in most cases prove ample when supplied by fans. The feeders may be cut away or left with an emergency handle attached, according to circumstances. In a two-manual organ the swell is, or should be, provided with a small separate reservoir underneath the swell sound-board. This is essential for steadiness, especially when playing detached chords on full swell or great. Where none exists, the tremulant, if there be one, will shake the whole organ instead of the swell manual, to which it alone belongs.

Next, the sound-board should be examined. I wish we could call them wind-chests, for the term is so misleading. Such builders as I have named invariably used fine, well-seasoned mahogany for the slides and upper-boards upon which the pipe feet rest. But unfortunately, side by side with excellent workmanship, one often finds the pipes crowded upon sound-boards measuring only about five feet. The bass octave of one or more of the 16ft. or 8ft. stops (not the reeds) may be removed, with perfectly good results, several feet away and placed upon a sound-board of their own. The pipes thus treated then require only a mere puff sufficient to actuate the pneumatic motors, the supply of wind which produces their speech coming through a separate wind trunk from bellows or reservoir to the new sound-board. If a new stop, or even two—provided they are not great wind-eaters—be required, a block may be added to the existing sound-board, a matter which requires too neat joinery to trust to any but most skilled hands.

Now in the ordinary church organs of such builders as I have named, and dating back, let us say, from thirty to seventy or eighty years, an expert would expect to find certain points of excellence, varying in degree, coupled with certain glaring shortcomings, which would cause persons unacquainted with the interior to condemn the whole. And only too often the whole has been swept away to make room for a cheap competition affair with defective tubular pneumatic work and altogether too much zinc.

Such organs as were erected before the age of zinc will probably have some good metal basses well worth retaining. Most of these old builders, too, put good material into their wood pipes, combined with neat workmanship in their stopped diapasons and bourdons, which, unless they happen to have suffered greatly from the ravages of worms, will be worth retaining. In the pedal opens, too, one often finds in cheap modein work thin pipes of much smaller scale which could be packed most comfortably, pipe for pipe, inside most of the opens built at a period when wood was not such a costly item to a builder.

In organs of the period we are now considering, the pedal will invariably be the weak part in the tonal scheme; a solitary pedal open, then a bourdon, then a principal 8ft. or violoncello were the gradations usually offered us in organs of varying size, in each case probably quite inadequate in firmness to the full organ it was supposed to balance. Even the best builders of the Victorian period were slow to realise that their pedal open and bourdon ought always to have been extended an octave to provide the much needed "binding" qualities of 8ft. basses, thus compensating, too, for the universal habit of grooving the dulciana of the great into a stopped wood bass and the open diapason of the swell in a similar manner. They never seemed to understand that an important pedal passage moving through full chords sustained by both hands should be firm and clear and not a mere rumble. One of the builders I have named made a special feature, at one period, of a crusade against tenor C work, carrying every stop through, combining this point with another good feature, —viz., a firm and ample wind supply. But these advantages were unfortunately counterbalanced by a most objectionable amount of zinc, even extending to the stopped pipes and harmonic flutes.

In another, one usually found some fine open diapasons of good round, satisfying tone, together with an excellent build-up to mixtures, combined with rather indifferent tracker-work and quite ordinary reeds. Another gave us in his small church organs a very inferior standard of metal to that of his more important instruments. Good sound workmanship and durability in the sound-boards and action with reeds of the very best, but with diapasons turned into gambas by slotting the pipes, were other features. Another made a point of using a good deal of pure tin. His stops, being thin, would be ill-adapted to modern wind pressures, but the best portions of such great and swell organs might often be preserved and made up into a useful choir organ on a light pressure. Yet another firm, now extinct, might invariably be recognised by its excellent clarabellas and mixtures, coarse reeds, " coughing " bourdons, diapasons always more or less of the "violin" diapason type, contra gambas as the swell double, with its 8ft. octave actually contriving "a double debt to pay " by appearing with very bad results as the bottom octave of the diapason.

If nearly all the shortcomings incidental to competitive organ building are evident in a particular instrument the only thing to be done is to dispose of it for what it will fetch to some less well-to-do community. Even so, carefully restored and rebuilt, it must be a very bad specimen indeed if it does not prove preferable to a harmonium for leading voices.

The Sound-Boards.

THE sound-boards — misleading name, since they are not sound-producing parts, but simply the wind-chests of compressed air upon which the pipes stand — are, nevertheless, the most vital parts of an organ, demanding the best of well-seasoned wood and most accurate workmanship, or the result is a failure to produce an efficient and playable instrument, no matter how good the pipework or the wind-supply. The table, slides and upper-boards should be of well-seasoned and carefully selected mahogany, skilfully planed and carefully adjusted, or they will prove a fruitful source of trouble. In the rainy season, the stops will work stiffly, and in very dry weather when they become free again there will be sundry hissing noises denoting wind escapes for which the pipes are sometimes unjustly blamed. The usual practice is to blacklead and polish the mahogany surfaces for smooth working; formerly the tables were leathered by the German builders and some English ones. Bishop and Holdich were perhaps the last to use leather. It was found to work badly with slides controlled pneumatically. The late Mr. Gern used moleskin, and in some of the Hope-Jones organs the surfaces are French polished and then rubbed over with French chalk, the greasy nature of which is well calculated to help the slides to run smoothly, although it cannot claim any advantage over blacklead.

To ease stiff slides, we must provide ourselves with a long screwdriver and find the holes placed at intervals along the rack-board which supports the pipes belonging to the particular stop affected.

These holes will be found to be directly over screws going through the upper-boards. Tightness is usually found at the extreme ends of a sound-board; these should be tried before disturbing the treble. By giving not more than half a turn to the left (or we may bring on "runnings"), and frequently testing the draw-stop, we shall be able to find where the fault lies. Should it become necessary to remove the pipes and take off both rack-board and upper-board entirely (involving the removal of two or more stops), the slide will show where it rubs hardest; and between each slide the little slips of wood known as bearers should have just at these points a thin strip of notepaper pasted down on each side. The slides, if they feel gritty, may be again rubbed down with blacklead and replaced, the other surfaces of course being carefully dusted before again screwing them down.

Before replacing the pipes, find out by frequent testings how much screwing down the upper-boards will bear. In extreme cases of warped wood, the only radical cure is for the organ builder to take the sound-board down and plane everything afresh, and of course only a man well skilled in the fine use of a plane can attempt such an operation.

Whilst such radical defects last, the unfortunate player has a choice of two evils: (1) screwing down the upper-boards so tight that a great strain is placed upon the draw-stops and composition pedal action; or (2) leaving things so slack that sundry wind escapes spoil the speech of the pipes. The scoring — i.e., little channels cut by a V-shaped tool, designed to take off any superfluous wind and prevent runnings from one note to another — will have of course to be deepened, should fresh planing have become necessary.

Runnings may also be traced to some defect in the grooves,—perhaps a slight crack in a sound-board bar, or a knot left uncovered. Or the bar itself may have become unglued, or the American cloth or parchment which covers the grooves underneath the sound-board at the back may be at fault.

There is a rough and ready method of curing runnings without taking down the sound-board — the objectionable practice known as "bleeding"— puncturing a small hole in the leather covering the groove; thereby releasing a little of the wind-supply instead of letting it enter the next groove. The fault is then converted into a hissing sound of escaping wind simultaneously with the speech of the pipe over that particular groove. Tuners will sometimes puncture these holes between the upper-tables, and then it is difficult to detect with all pipes in place. When a new sound-board shows any signs of runnings and it is found that the upper-boards will not admit of being screwed down any tighter upon the slides, it is the builder's obvious duty to take the sound-board down and treat it thoroughly after the manner I have indicated.

When there is doubt about the soundness of the bars (some builders have even screwed as well as glued them into their places, to be quite safe), the grooves underneath are stripped of their leather and all the wind-holes filled with temporary wooden wedges. (Pieces of various sized trackers are often cut up for this purpose.) The sound-board is then turned upside down, the pallets having been removed, and thin hot glue is poured into the grooves, one or two only at a time, until nearly level. It is allowed a few moments to search its way into any possible cracks, and then the wedges are withdrawn and the glue allowed to drain off into a pan underneath. Subsequently, of course, all the upper surface must be planed over afresh. This operation is known to builders as "flooding."

Once done, it is a permanent safeguard against further trouble; but it is obviously a disagreeable operation, and to be regarded as a last resort.

When pneumatic action has to be fitted to slider sound-boards, it is of the utmost importance that the slides shall move quite freely, or the motors will not be able to overcome promptly the resistance offered.

Should it be necessary to renew the springs, steel piano wire is preferable to brass. Weak springs may be stiffened by pulling them further apart, but the tips must not be pulled out of line with each other. A good preservative against rust in damp localities is a little vaseline smeared over a piece of flannel. the springs being lightly rubbed over before replacing. After twenty or thirty years' use, the leather and felt facings of the pallets will have become hard and noisy, when they should be removed, stripped and placed side by side. A strip of new leather and felt of a corresponding length having been obtained from one of the supply dealers, the pallets are glued one by one and pressed down upon it; a board with a weight upon it securing the whole until dry. Next day, each pallet may be cut out with a sharp knife. They are then surfaced by rubbing face downward on a level board sprinkled with whitening; this to make them perfectly even, so that they may "bed" accurately. As a help to this end, it is sometimes desirable in new work to put in stiff springs at first (especially in damp situations, where ciphering is feared), afterwards lightening the touch with weaker springs when it is considered safe to do so.

Defective pallets are a serious trouble. If builders would only use pin-pallets, or hinge them as in American organs so that each one could be removed singly, much subsequent annoyance would be spared the player. It is a serious matter to have to remove all the pipes from a large sound-board, especially when there is a great deal of convey-ancing and so much of the organ has been built around it. It is strange that no builder has ever thought of screwing a narrow board underneath the whole length of the sound-board, just under the tail of the pallets, similar to the front-boards. They could then be reached easily to correct a fault or to re-cover a whole set without having to turn the sound-board upside down.

It must be noted that they are graduated in size and accurately refilled to cover their respective grooves; whether pin pallets (which are preferable) or secured in the old-fashioned way by a strip of wood nailed down over all the tail ends, which by the way must not be "hinge bound." In order to secure a minimum of noise, builders have tried a very soft woolly felt underneath a strip of hard-leather facing; but this sometimes causes trouble by curling up in the middle, when the player dis-covers on drawing some such stop as the fifteenth, which is prompt to speak on a light wind-supply, that there are sundry unaccountable whimperings, increasing or diminishing according to the varying climatic conditions.

When a pallet closes badly, the resultant cipher-ing is most noticeable when a stop is drawn re-quiring the least amount of wind to cause it to speak, such as a 2ft. stop. Before unscrewing the face-board, a possible cause may be found in a bent or rusty pull-down. If not here, there may be grit on the leathered surface, or the pallet spring may be too weak or out of position, or the guide-pins may be holding it too tight, or the pallet leather may have curled up in the centre.

A pallet-cleaning tool may be easily made from a thin strip of wood about a foot long and half-an-inch wide, with a piece of velvet glued to the end. Pull down the pallet and insert the tool, drawing it from back to front. If the upper surface of leather has become detached from the felt, it may be refastened with seccotine. The upper surface should then be well smoothed out with the newly made tool (or the reed tuning-knife will serve), for unless it "beds" very accurately we shall effect no cure, but rather make matters worse.

The pallet guard is a thin strip of wood "sprung" into grooves at the ends of the sound-board and covered with a strip of cloth or felt—or it may be screwed to the face-board—with the object of preventing the pallet from being pulled down too far. It is altogether too tedious an operation to attempt the removal of the pallet springs without a special tool, and this is a long strip of iron terminating in a Y shape, the extremities being turned over so as to grip the spring. A little practice will enable any handy man to use it to remove faulty or broken springs. It will be noted that both ends of the spring must fit into the holes made for that purpose. The comb or register through which the spring moves is to prevent any side shifting. If stouter springs have to be substituted, it may be necessary to enlarge these openings with a flat file. Guide pins are pieces of wire placed each side of the pallet to direct it into the way it should go in obedience to the impulse from the key. The pull-downs work through a brass plate either let into the under-board (as was Robson's practice) or secured underneath it with strips of wood each side, the object being equally attained in either case of preventing any accidental bending of the wire. If the holes have become enlarged through long use, hissing noises will be heard, and it will be desirable to substitute stouter wire for the pull-downs. Metal working against metal is best lubricated with vaseline. Sometimes the setting-out of the roller-arms in relation to the pull-downs is all askew ; and if the objectionable side-pull thus set up has worn away the holes in the brass plate to any extent, a new one should be substituted. "Split" pallets are of course to be preferred in all but the smallest organs to ease the touch, and any sound old set may be thus treated before being replaced. With such there is not so much surface resistance on depressing a key, and a pleasanter feeling is imparted to the touch. Our renovated sound-board, if originally well made, should be good for another quarter-of-a-century's work.

Unfortunately, with the thrusting of organs into chambers and chancel positions unsuited to them, the roomy sound-boards often found in old organs of Snetzler's period, built for west-end galleries, were abandoned by our English builders; and their excellent workmanship had the serious defect of overcrowding in the tenor and middle octaves. Their employers thought it a mark of cleverness to be able to squeeze into five or six feet stops formerly spread over eight or nine feet. Thus a false measurement was set up, and the tone of the diapasons and reeds, especially, suffered through actually touching each other, or the flue pipes speaking direct into each other's mouths. It would be well if we could have as a rough and ready rule for all new work some such agreement as this: no pipe to have less clear space than its diameter (or depth) in front of its mouth. It is very annoying to find, in an otherwise excellent sound-board, that it is impossible to increase the scale of any given stop, however desirable it may be tonally. Many an unwise enlargement scheme has been forced upon a reluctant or too accommodating builder by enthusiastic amateurs, really defeating its own ends. No one is competent to order this or that stop to be replaced on a sound-board by something that seems more desirable, unless he is conversant with the scale of the stop; the space and the amount of wind it will take.

There is no real gain if we crowd in some large scale stop so that the pipes have no breathing room, at the same time blocking the free egress of tone from the stops behind it. There should always, too, be a passage-board of not less than one foot down the middle, excepting, of course, on small sound-boards where the pipes are arranged semi - tonally. Ample wind trunks and deep grooves are points which the reader is advised to note in all really high class work which he may be privileged to examine. Though written many years ago in the late T. C. Lewis's book on organ building, the following remarks, by H. S., are worth quoting to-day :—

"An organ of specified size, made by a builder of high class work, would possess a sound-board to the great organ of measurement 8ft. 6in. by 4ft. and 12in. deep. By a second-rate maker, the same would be reduced in measurement to 6ft. by 4ft. with a depth of only $8\frac{1}{2}$in. In the frame work and supports we should find the bearing - rails and cross-rails 7in. by 2in., instead of 9in. by 3in.; the posts perhaps 4in. by 3in., instead of $4\frac{1}{2}$in. by 4in.; the levers actuating the sliders 3in. by $\frac{3}{4}$in., instead of $5\frac{1}{2}$in. by 1in.; wind trunks 12in. by 12in., reduced to 9in. by 9in.; squares that should be 4in., cut down to an insignificant $2\frac{3}{4}$in. The swell sound-board would be in like manner reduced in all its proportions, the swell box be small in size, packed with stunted, mitred pipes, and formed of wood $1\frac{1}{2}$in. in thickness, when at least 2in. is desirable. The bellows also of only $1\frac{1}{2}$in. stuff, when 2in. is necessary for solidity and steadiness, and whereas a good bellows for the instrument cited would have a superficies of 50ft. and a rise of 12in., the cheap style would give only about 35ft., with a rise of 7in."

Young enthusiasts who are fond of reading and drawing up fancy specifications would do well also to think over the same writer's remarks on the "occult attraction, the fascination exercised by names over men's affections," for they could hardly be improved upon :—

"Men invoke names with something of the faith of the old magicians, that the power they call will come forth at command. If a stop is labelled 'diapason,' it is believed, without question, that the diapason tone is behind it, when, in reality, the quality is perhaps only as of a larger flute, and not the quality a master in scaling and voicing would admit to be a diapason at all. The quality of stops should be tested by the ear, rather than by the stop-knobs......Fancy stops are often highly prized solely for their names: and, not infrequently, one builder gains an advantage over others by inserting in his specification 'a pretty stop' which is eagerly caught at and marked off, like a lot in an auctioneer's catalogue, to be secured at any cost."

The Rack-Boards.

IN badly built or ill-cared for organs, we shall probably find serious faults here. For correct speech and also for the preservation of the pipes, it is essential that every pipe should be accurately fitted into its particular hole, so that it will not shift during the process of tuning. If they are allowed to roll about through any of the holes being too large, an accidental touch will put them quite out of tune, especially the reeds, whose boots should be so firm that in knocking up the wires they will remain immovable. Reed boots, in fact, are best left undisturbed until a general cleaning of the whole of the pipes on the sound-board becomes necessary. Too often one finds split rack-boards, covered with grit and dust and plentiful droppings of candlegrease by careless tuners. Wherever possible, a portable electric light should be provided, and the use of candles strictly prohibited, for the " organ-builder's candle " (commonly a bit of candle fastened into a small square of wood) has occasioned many a disastrous fire. I have often seen charred woodwork inside an organ,—evidence of some narrow escape.

Frequently, when stops have been changed, we shall find evidence of hasty work and badly fitted pipes. The scale probably varying a little, they may be either squeezed in, bruising the feet, or loosely dropped in, when the act of coning, in the case of small pipes, means twisted feet and eventual ruin, through the pipes not receiving support just where it is most needed. Often a small pipe has been put off its speech altogether through the mouth being driven in. The remedy is to take it out and roll it gently on a board until it is straightened out. The rack-board holes, when too large for the feet of flue pipes or the boots of reeds, should be leathered around with strips of white leather, which may be quite well put in with seccotine, and then greased. Rack pillars are sometimes screwed in and provided with a wooden nut on top. Ordinary pine is generally considered good enough for the rack-boards, but Mr. Lewis often used cedar. The upper surface should receive a coat of varnish, but too seldom gets it. If it is necessary to file any of the holes to ensure a better fit, a round file must be procured, and a piece of paper pushed underneath to prevent the filed particles of wood from dropping through the footholes and on to the pallets. It is usual to divide the rack-boards and upper-board so that each will carry two or three stops only. When a new stop has to be fitted, this portion only need be removed. Unscrewing the upper-boards exposes the sliders, which of course may be at the same time taken out and cleaned, or freshly black-leaded if it seems necessary. At any rate they should be carefully wiped over before replacing lest any grit prevent the smooth working of the draw stop. With upper-board and rack-boards set up temporarily upon a table or panel laid across some seats, the pipes may be easily adjusted to their respective holes.

Restoration of the Pipes.

IF any reader interested in this subject has had no previous experience in handling pipes he would be well advised to procure a few odd ones—any small metal pipes will do—and experiment with them, so as to test for himself the effect of alterations to the upper lip, windway, foothole or languid, before touching those in the organ itself. If he is neat-handed and possesses a keen ear, he may confidently expect to acquire a fair knowledge of the art of regulating. Having thus previously experimented, he will gradually become more certain of his ground in dealing with any given stop that calls for improvement. But the keen ear must become educated by frequently comparing the tone of stops by a great variety of builders, if he aims at really artistic results and not a mere workman's job of the commercial type.

Now metal pipes are long suffering, and if originally well made they need not lightly be discarded to make room for new merely on account of their present unsatisfactory tone or faulty regulation. Bruises can be rounded out; the set of the upper lip, lower lip and languid corrected; evenness as to power secured by reducing or enlarging the foothole : ragged tops (most detrimental to tone) trimmed and provided with tinned slides, and, within reasonable limits, the whole stop loudened or softened. A careful inspection of each stop should first be made to ascertain if materials and workmanship were originally good. If the wood pipes are quite worm-eaten and the metal ones too thin to bear handling, or the whole of rough workmanship, their fate is quickly decided ; but if originally good, the probabilities are that careful restoration and re-voicing will improve them beyond all recognition. If the organ has fallen into bad hands, the metal pipes will probably be much bruised, torn and pinched at the top, with their feet bent through the action of the cone in tuning pipes that should first have had their tops neatly trimmed and put into condition, so that only a slight touch of the cone would have been needed, Bruises may be pressed out by any long round piece of wood or metal of suitable diameter, which must not be pushed in so far as to disturb the "set" of the upper lip,

Tin Slides.

FROM any tinsmith pieces of tinplate can be procured, cut into suitable sizes and rounded to fit the pipes. The edges of the slides must of course slightly overlap, or we should produce the kind of tone associated with slotted pipes. Small pipes less than half-an-inch in diameter are best tuned with the cone ; and if over three inches, a wide slot near the top is usually made. Most tuners, too, would, I think, prefer to have no slides for the principal and mixture stops ; these should be cut to the right size for their respective notes with especial care and accuracy, ultimately a trifle on the " sharp " side, that they may be flattened by coning the tops in. With these reservations, tuning slides should be universally applied, as the best way of preserving the pipes, also with the object of preserving the regulation ; for, when cones are exclusively used, to flatten a pipe by coning the top inward also tends to soften. To sharpen the pipe by coning the top outward tends to louden, so that a stop will gradually get out of regulation from frequent tunings, whereas neatly fitted tuning slides will preserve permanently the symmetry of the pipes. Pinched or torn tops spoil the purity of tone ; so will bad bruises, or anything in fact that interferes with the smooth cylindrical outline of the pipes.

Tinplates, of course, are made in varying thicknesses, and a little commonsense will be needed to gauge the slides to the diameter of the pipe. They should be from one to two or three inches in width, slightly overlapping, and when sprung on properly there need be no fear of a slide becoming loose and slipping down the pipe. They are easily made and rolled over anything round,—a pencil, a ruler, a broom handle, lengths of curtain pole in brass or wood, all come in useful to give a series of graduated diameters. The pipes are of course cut down slightly, sharpening them, so that the slides may project a little at the top for the purpose of tuning, which may be effected with a reed-knife, screwdriver or chisel.

The "spring" given to the tuning slide must not squeeze the pipe so hard that the act of knocking-up the slide to flatten will knock it out of its hole. Here again we see the importance of fitting every pipe firmly in the rack-board, else tuning is much hindered and cannot be so accurate if we have to handle the pipes during the process.

Unscrupulous builders are not likely to advocate the use of slides; it is so much "better for trade" that the old pipe-work should be condemned *en bloc*, allowed for at the price of old metal and used elsewhere in a rebuild! From their standpoint, it is inexpedient that an organ should be made to last too long and its tuning facilitated.

Organists who are not very familiar with the interior of their organs should endeavour to make themselves so; proceeding to do so cautiously and not disturbing pipes (particularly reeds) for examination until by observation and advice they understand how to handle them. A quiet examination of the tops of the pipes will soon show whether the tuning has been in good hands or not. The writer has seen in an organ not a year old, which had been entirely under the "care" (!) of the original builder, pipes pinched three-corner shape at the top, as if the tuner had been too lazy to bring his tuning cones with him. When pipes are thus treated, the regulation greatly suffers;

and a stop which may have left the voicer's hands in good order will naturally sound rough and uneven.

Increase in Scale.

A STOP may be completely altered in character by a very simple method of increasing the " scale," shifting up an entire set one or more notes, cutting and trimming the tops to the new pitch of each note. Broadly speaking, narrow scales imply a thinner, smaller tone with a tendency to stringiness ; pipes wider of diameter, fuller tone, with a tendency to flutiness ; if greatly exaggerated, to dulness. The narrow scales bring into greater prominence the upper partials, which sound along with the fundamental note and give the stop its special character. Thus the gamba class, and particularly the keen-toned modern viols, are the smallest of the foundation stops in diameter and present the strongest possible contrast to the very large scale open diapasons found in modern organs, — contrasts which would certainly have greatly surprised the old builders. The viols have been reduced to a diameter of $1\frac{1}{16}$ in. at CC, and the opens increased to 9in. in some extreme cases ; whereas 3in. was formerly considered narrow enough for any string-toned gamba, and $6\frac{1}{4}$in. a fair normal average of the large great organ diapason. It is, then, in the judicious choice of suitable scales as much as in the ultimate care with which they are treated that the voicer can show his artistic feeling.

In thus shifting up a set of pipes, we must of course order from a pipe maker one or more new pipes for the bottom notes, sending the former CC or tenor C as a pattern. This shifting up is often desirable, too, when it is decided to raise the wind pressure in a reconstructed organ, for there is naturally a considerable difference between what we may term " chamber organ " scales and those suited to a large and powerful organ. If the sound-board is to be used again, we must of course see what space can be allowed for the increase, paying special attention to the bass and tenor octaves, for it is in these that overcrowding mostly occurs.

Repairs to Tracker Work.

I T will be of service to enumerate here the articles necessary for the repairer to have always at hand. They are: a screwdriver, a tube of seccotine, a few tapped wires, a few pieces of tracker, some leather buttons, red cloths for same, carpet thread, a reed tuning knife, and brass tuning cones. If slides are fitted to all but the smaller pipes only one cone may be needed. The Hope-Jones organs in which mixtures find no place, are fitted throughout with slides, and in these cones are dispensed with entirely. Tinned slides certainly do prolong the life of the pipes by retaining the original regulation, but it is obvious that very neat and accurate fitting is required when applying them to pipes no larger than a slate pencil. The advertisements of the supply houses will indicate where the foregoing requisites, which are not sold locally, may be obtained, and the articles (with the exception of a complete set of brass cones) are quite inexpensive. How much an amateur may attempt must depend on his local conditions. Unless there exists a contract placing the services of a tuner always at his command, he should at least be able to repair a broken tracker (if fairly accessible), cure a simple cipher, replace a loose button, or tune a few pipes which from some cause are violently out of tune, or any such simple matter requiring only a little commonsense and a certain neatness of hand, best acquired by watching a good workman. For anything to do with reeds (the most delicate and easily injured portion of an organ), any hints to be given later on should be supplemented by actual demonstration by a good tuner.

The Trackers.

IN old organs, the tapped wires, being of brass, are a frequent source of trouble, becoming green with corrosion and liable to snap when one attempts to turn a button. Unravelling the thread from a broken wire will show how the pointed end of the tracker is shaped by a penknife, and how the carpet thread is bound around, beginning at the pointed end; the bent end of the tapped wire being pressed through a hole made with a fine bradawl. To prevent the thread from unravelling, it is treated with thin glue or seccotine; or, if an entirely new set of trackers is to be made, they should be varnished, and the varnish will be sufficient to keep the thread in place. The brass-tapped wires in use fifty years ago were superseded by tinned iron; these are strong, but liable to rust, and have been in their turn supplanted by phosphor bronze. A little pure tallow (obtainable from the ironmonger) or a pot of vaseline should always be kept at hand, and no button should ever be put on without dipping the end of the tapped wire into this. Buttons which cannot be turned without risk of a breakage may be eased by squeezing them all round with a pair of pliers and greasing the corroded wire over which they are to pass.

To ensure a quiet action, it is well to put double cloths (unless they are fairly thick), and in certain cases double buttons, — one on each side of the arm, backfall or square. But when this is done, they should not be screwed up tight; it should be possible to move the tracker round. Remember always to put the rounded end of the button against the moving part, not *vice versâ*, as might seem more natural to a novice. Since the movement is at an angle, the reason will be obvious on a little consideration.

It will be noted that in old organs the trackers are square and vary very greatly in thickness. They are more liable to split and are less neat in appearance than the round trackers now always used. Wire is inadmissible for two reasons; there is no grip for the fingers when turning a button, and if of any length metal is subject to lengthening and shortening under the influence of heat and cold, so that the touch would become irregular with each considerable change of temperature. As the player's comfort and security is dependent upon hundreds of these insignificant little buttons, one should never permit a loose one to remain. Properly fitted, they will retain their grip for almost a lifetime under reasonable conditions.

Many a fault in the foregoing little details connected with tracker work is traceable to some organ-builder's careless apprentice, who needs constant supervision lest he mar otherwise good work!

Backfalls and Squares.

THESE transmit the movement at a different angle. They should be of hard wood, —mahogany or oak—and well seasoned material is of great importance. In old work, it will probably be found that the centres are not bushed with cloth. This should be attended to: rusty pins drawn out and replaced with phosphor bronze. The sides, if there is too much loose "play," are papered and again black-leaded. If the original work is bad, fresh squares in a new mahogany stock may be necessary in order to get a perfect and reliable touch.

When metal squares were first introduced in place of wood, they were made of brass, with the centres not bushed; and, becoming corroded in time, especially where much gas is used, are a very common cause of that vexatious non-return of key known as a cipher. In modern work, white metal or phosphor bronze is used, and the centres are neatly bushed with cloth as in any good piano action. It is obviously an advantage to be able to unscrew each square separately, instead of having to deal with a long pin running through the entire set, as in the older builders' wooden squares. A broken wooden square, if it is too much trouble to draw out the pin holding the entire set in place, may usually be repaired with thin pieces of hard wood neatly fastened across the fracture with seccotine. Or the pin may be filed through and a new square substituted. Where trouble of this kind is frequently arising, a few white metal squares should be kept: they are made in two or three sizes. Wooden squares are, or should be, in two pieces, dovetailed across the grain, and not cut off a single piece of wood, as has sometimes been done for the sake of cheapness. The reader will now begin to realise how interdependent are the various moving parts of an organ, and the need for perfect accuracy in every detail if we are to obtain a quiet and pleasant working of the whole. Actions allowed to become very loose will not take down the pallets to their full extent, so that we do not get the full speech of the pipe.

The Roller-Boards.

IF the organ is more than half-a-century old we shall find wooden roller-boards occupying a great deal more space than is necessary, and blocking off much light from the interior.   Much of the clatter in a noisy action may be traced to them. The pins have become too "free," and the arms have probably lost their bushings.   Though an improvement may be made by substituting stouter pins, it is seldom a wise economy.   It is much better to discard them in favour of iron, occupying about half the space, besides being quieter in action.   So with trundles of composition action : though hard wood is frequently found, iron is best, both for rigidity and the saving of space,—always a point to consider in organ work, the combined economy of space and superior efficiency being so much to the good.

In ordinary composition actions, iron fans running through the upright iron trundles will be noticed. On pressing down a composition pedal, its fan will push out certain stops and push in others by pressure against little wooden blocks about an inch square and bushed with felt to prevent noise. If the action of the pedal is unequal, leaving some stop partly thrown out and another not fully sent home, the remedy will be obvious if the action is watched whilst someone moves the pedal, and a piece or two of felt of suitable thickness applied where the failure occurs will soon set matters right. These iron compositions are, or should be, set in a hard wood frame. If the sockets in which they work have become enlarged with use, the only effectual remedy is to have the whole frame taken out and reset, when the opportunity might be taken of effecting an entire reconstruction of the means of control if the composition pedals are too few, as is the case in so many old organs.

Regulation of the Tracker-Work.

TOUCH in tracker organs alters considerably under changes of atmospheric conditions, due to the expansion and contraction of wood and metal, long actions being naturally more affected than those which are quite simple and direct. The tendency is towards shallowness of touch in a hot, dry summer, the touch deepening again in cold, wet weather. A flimsy building frame, built of unseasoned wood, is a fruitful source of trouble in this direction. Organ builders should provide back-falls, from whence the manual touch is raised or lowered with a thumb-screw at each end, thus enabling one instantly to alter the whole level an eighth of an inch or more to the correct depth (three-eighths of an inch), after which it is an easy matter to take off a cipher or two at the arm underneath the pull-downs. When every note has to be altered separately the thumper is raised temporarily by wedging up the highest and lowest keys—these are left until last to regulate—and a slip of hard wood with a perfectly straight edge is of service to secure a good level. When keys are "cast"—i.e., twisted a little on one side—as in many old organs, it is not possible to secure a perfect line, but we must adjust the [differences as best we may. Tracker work is capable of a great variety of treatment in various details in laying out an action, and an organ by some builder whose work is the result of a different set of workmen with entirely different traditions is certain to present some interesting differences of treatment.

The best plan, therefore, is for the organist to make a sketch giving a side-view of the action of one key of any organ he wishes to understand thoroughly; it will often be of use in tracing any fault to its source,—frequently a puzzling matter to those who do not profess to be skilled mechanics. It makes all the difference in favour of a full, firm speech from the pipes when the pallets open to their full extent, and this cannot be the case when the touch has become "fleet" (as some workmen term shallow touch), nor should tuning be attempted under such unfavourable conditions. Before leaving a newly regulated action, test for cipherings with the stop on each key-board which requires least wind, such as a 2ft.; when any slight tendency to cipher owing to the first inrush of wind, causing some pallet to open slightly, may be rectified. Also test with couplers drawn. Octave and sub-octave couplers in tracker work require the most careful adjusting, and the fewer of these in such organs the better; whereas in pneumatic, and still more in electric, work the builder has a ready means of making an apparently large organ out of a very limited number of real speaking stops.

Cleaning the Metal Pipes.

METAL pipes should be taken out, and the small ones laid down very carefully to avoid injury to the mouth and ears of the delicate rollers or freins of viols and gambas. The larger ones (unless of zinc) should be placed upside down against a wall to prevent flattening. In cleaning, use a soft camel's hair brush for the mouths of all small pipes, and for the inside a piece of rag or a duster tied to sticks of varying length, or a bottle brush will serve the purpose. Metal pipes may be finally rinsed out in a large tray of water, standing them upside down to dry, but we must be careful not to allow the windway to become choked and dust in the nicking converted into mud : for very little dust suffices to impair and even silence the speech of small mixtures and viols,—in fact the latter on account of the freins should not be so treated. The original appearance of the metal may be restored by rubbing the pipes with whiting upon chamois leather ; the durability of the brightness thus regained will vary considerably with the proportion of tin to lead, and also as to the locality, —i.e., whether the organ is in the country or in some manufacturing town, or specially affected by gaslighting and heating. Gilt or diapered fronts may be sponged over with cold water, but the gilt should afterwards receive a coating of size,— i.e., very thin glue.

Wood Pipes.

THESE may of course be piled freely on one another. Examine for worm holes, and if any are found apply paraffin to each hole with a fine brush. Violin dealers make a mixture of resin and beeswax melted and neatly dropped into each hole—a piece of match will serve—smoothing it off instantly while liquid. These little hard-shell pests are especially fond of walnut and any unseasoned wood, and in rooms where they have made inroads into the furniture may often be found on the ceilings in August, when they develop rudimentary wings, taking short and clumsy flights and spreading rapidly unless checked. All wood pipes should be either sized and varnished or painted. The red sizing formerly used so much for cheapness comes off too freely and is not to be recommended. It may be washed off if desired, and the pipes given a suitable coating of paint of a red-brown shade, the original sizing serving as a first coat or priming. If the pipes have not been treated by either paint or varnish, it is worth while, both for the preservation of the wood and for appearance, to remedy this omission.

Whilst the wood pipes are out of the organ, all stoppers should be examined. They are (or should be) with the exception of the adjustable cork-lined stoppers, covered with substantial white leather, glued only to the flat part. Between the leather and the wood at the sides, insert a strip of brown paper if the stoppers are loose ; and if they do not move freely, rub a little pure tallow against the leather at the sides. The stopper may be got out by knocking one end down with a hammer, taking care not to knock it into the pipe so that its handle cannot be reached. Leave them flat—merely inserted at the top—for subsequent tuning. Small wooden pipes have their caps glued on, while larger ones are screwed. It is seldom necessary to remove a cap; but makers have sometimes been known to leave chips inside, and these getting lodged in the windway spoil the speech.

It is a curious fact that a pipe which is a little narrower towards the middle than at the top and bottom will give a note of poor quality. In making large wooden opens and bourdons, as the sides are being nailed and glued together, some pieces of wood are lightly nailed inside to prevent any tendency of this kind; when the pipes are finished they are, of course, knocked out. Through carelessness, in a Robson organ these "try pieces" remained for twenty-five years until discovered by a local builder in nearly all the pedal opens, when they were knocked out by letting a heavy sash-weight tied to a rope down the pipe, the pieces of wood being removed through the mouth of the pipe. A subsequent examination of the bass octaves of the bourdon and the great and swell doubles brought to light a great many more. Thus for the first quarter of a century of its existence, the proper tone of the wood basses in this particular organ had never been heard by anyone, and it is quite possible that there may still exist similar cases of oversight.

In some old organs these wood basses have been cut down too short by mistake. If it is not expedient to shift them all up one note (supplying a new pipe for the lowest note, and cutting down afresh, they should be lengthened an inch or two with new wood neatly dowelled and glued to the top and **V** shaped saw-cuts made in front, with a slide screwed on for tuning purposes. The screw should slant a little downward : this will bind the top of the slide tighter against the pipe, else the vibration may set up a jarring noise. When, owing to an open wood pipe being too short it has to be flattened by screwing a piece of wood across the top, such partial closing naturally weakens the tone and puts it out of regulation with the rest.

Stopped pipes that are too short are more difficult to treat, as the interior of the added parts must be absolutely flush with the rest of the pipe. But the following remedies may be tried, each tending to flatten the note : —

1. The addition of ears and beard.

2. A thin piece of book-binder's leather seccotined round the upper lip.

3. More plugging at the foot, if it will bear softening.

4. A thin slip of wood each side of the windway, slightly reducing its width by closing it.

These are more or less "fakes,"—useful as a last resort in bad cases, and of two evils one chooses the least. It is certainly better to endure a little unevenness in tone as to power or quality than to have a note or two which cannot be put in tune.

Bourdons often give great trouble before a perfectly even tone is obtained. Each note should be soft, yet pure and pervading, with an agreeable humming undertone. When this is lacking and the tone of an apparently well made pipe is thin and poor, the fault may lie in the cap being set a trifle too low against the block. A glued cap may be knocked off with a smart blow of a hammer to rectify this fault.

The inside edge of the upper lip should not be rounded, and it should be quite parallel with the block. It is either left square or slightly bevelled outwards. In small organs containing only **one** 16ft. stop it may be thought desirable to leave **a** little of the "bite" which a thick and low **upper** lip will give. When the upper lips have **been** spoilt by being badly cut up and the tone is consequently poor and uneven, if the pipes are **in** other respects well made, a good stop can usually be made of it by cutting out the whole of **the** upper lips and neatly inserting new ones of **hard** wood, cautiously cutting up afresh a little at **a** time on its own wind until the true bourdon quality is obtained.

The Material of Pipes.

WOODEN pipes are mostly made of **well** seasoned pine, as even in grain and **as** free from knots as possible. In organs of the Victorian period, an **excellent** even-grained red pine is much in evidence; **but** the supply gradually ceased. Occasionally **one** meets with small wooden pipes made of mahogany, and in very old organs sometimes of oak. **It** is found desirable in large pedal pipes to **insert** oak upper lips.

The metal pipes are mostly a compound of **lead** and tin in varying proportions. "Plain metal"— 75% lead to 25% tin — is excellent for the diapasons, but the feet of the bass octave must **be** hardened, to withstand the weight, by a slight admixture of antimony. All string-toned stops **are** best in spotted metal or pure tin, and it is by **no** means a waste of money (when it can be afforded) to have those reeds from which we require **a** special brilliance to be of spotted metal, — **by** which is generally understood a mixture of tin **and** lead in nearly equal proportions. For keen **viols,** pure tin—which should be virgin tin, not meltings-down—should be used for durability as well as for tone on account of their slender scale.

Zinc, if of the hard-rolled kind (as supplied by Kitsell), is excellent for 16ft. octaves, and also for the 8ft. octaves of gambas; but above that the tone seems "tight," lacks weight and does not yield so musical a quality as plain metal. Wherever it is used, the lips should be of spotted metal, or good voicing will be impracticable. Certain builders, not knowing how to treat zinc, have resorted to baking it to obtain pliability. The result is a worthless material, which is liable to crumble and break away. There also exists a cheap quality of zinc which no builder who values his reputation would think of using. So liable is it to corrosion that it is less durable than the commonest lead castings.

Every possible material has been experimented with in the manufacture of organ pipes,— gold, silver, ivory, bamboo and paper; but nothing is ever likely to supersede the admixture of tin and lead. Each of these possesses the defects of its qualities. Lead gives weight of tone; in excess, dulness and lack of durability; tin gives bright-ness. But if only tin were used for all the metal pipes (unless the foundation work were made of extra thick sheets at great cost), the general effect would be too shrill. Zinc is greatly lacking in richness of tone and carrying power, and should never be tolerated in any stop above 8ft. C.

Cleaning the Reeds.

I N the case of large pipes lift the tube out of the socket above the tuning wire and lay it aside, upside down. Then remove the part containing the reed from the boot. The tuning wire is then pushed down over the tongue, and the little wooden wedge pulled out with the point of a penknife or a bradawl. The barrel, reed, or shallot, as it is variously termed, may then be brushed out, and its face burnished if necessary by rubbing on a smooth and level piece of wood. The tongue should be wiped over. If it needs burnishing, the greatest care must be taken not to alter the original curvature in the slightest degree. If the curvature is lessened, a weak, inferior tone will result; if widened, it will be slower in speech. The tubes may be cleaned with a wire mop or long bottle brush. In removing a whole set of reeds, take care to lay them down in regular order in some safe place. The rack-board and upper-board should be cleaned at the same time, and every key must be well pressed down, with the reed stops drawn, to blow away any dust which may have dropped on the pallets. It is better to clean these also before replacing the reeds, by unscrewing the front of the sound-board and passing a thin flat piece of wood, covered with a piece of velvet or cloth, down each pallet from back to front. The learner will quickly discover how tiny a speck of dust is sufficient to silence or spoil the tone of any reed pipe, and he will soon learn to recognise the symptoms in a roughness of

tone. When tuning, by knocking the tuning wire
up sharply, these minute particles of dirt will usually fall, though they will still be there to give
trouble on some possible future occasion. Trumpet
stops are often "hooded" to prevent dust falling
straight down the tubes. Messrs. Walker close the
tops of their oboes, making circular openings
round the sides of the tubes at the top.   They also
protect the choir clarinets by entirely covering
them with thin panels of wood, providing a little
cloth screen or blind in front of the tuning wires
to exclude dust from the rack-board.   In some of
Messrs. Beal & Thynne's organs little discs of
gauze wire were dropped down the tubes to prevent the dust reaching the tongue.   But these
discs would in time become loaded with dust and
alter the speech of the pipes by muffling the tone.
And dust is just as likely to be drawn in through
feeders and wind - trunks. Mr. T. C. Lewis tried
placing fine copper wire gauze outside the valves,
and sometimes one finds a thin board placed over
a set of open reed tubes to exclude dust from the
ceiling.   Since dust is the great enemy of reeds, it
would be well if churches were provided with that
useful invention of an organ builder,—the vacuum
cleaner, which eats up the enemy without allowing any particles to float about as in the usual
cleaning operations.

When replacing the shallots, it will be seen
that a notch in the brass indicates how far it must
be pushed into the block.   The flattened face of
the shallot must be parallel with the straight edge
of the block; and the wedge, a little pointed piece
of hard wood, should secure the narrow end of the
tongue firmly, and this in turn must be fitted with
absolute exactness when passing the tuning wire
over it.

The Front Pipes.

FAULTS in the speech of the front pipes may often be traced to leakage in the wind supply through the conveyances between them and the sound - board. The joints of conveyances should be "knuckled," so as to avoid the check to the wind supply which results when, to save time in mitreing and soldering, right angles are made. They should be well fitted, to prevent wind escapes, as it is very annoying to find one accidentally pushed out of its hole on the sound-board in some difficult position, necessitating the removal of many pipes to put it right again. Small tubing is best secured either with seccotine or with "Chatterton's Compound," as used by the electricians, and to be bought in sticks. It can be melted at the flame of a candle, like sealing-wax, but never becomes hard enough to chip off, like ordinary glue does; it is easily melted up again, and a conveyance can be pulled out again with less danger of bruising it or breaking a joint. A little practice in twisting the melted end of the stick around the end of the tubing will soon enable the amateur to make a neat "collar." Large zinc trunks are best secured with tow and glue, and should be fitted into a collar or block which may be unscrewed. Sometimes a wooden frame-work is made, partitioned off into grooves about an inch square, with a short piece of tubing run out from the ends into the block under the pipe foot.

Robbing.

SMALL, overcrowded sound-boards, shallow grooves, wind escapes, and the substitution of stops demanding more wind are the chief causes of this defect. The tuner finds that, however careful he may have been in working with each individual stop and the principal, when the whole of the stops on the sound-board are drawn the trebles are flat and the speech unsteady. If we have to use the same sound-board we can effect a great improvement by the use of tubular pneumatics for the bass octave of the double, if any, and the open diapasons, with the additional advantage of being able to group them in some more favourable position, and so relieve the overcrowding at the same time. The wind supply for the pipes thus treated comes of course through a separate tube or trunk from reservoir or bellows, the only demand from the sound-board itself being the mere puff of air required to move the valve or motor which opens the pallet.

The Speech of Pipes.

THE relative *power* of tone in any given pipe depends first on the wind pressure and then again on the size of the foot-hole, which determines how much is admitted into the pipe. Its *quality* or character depends on many things,—the material of which it is made, the thickness of that material, the fineness or coarseness of the nicking, the height of the upper lip, the width of the mouth, as well as the "scale" or diameter of the pipe itself. Speech is caused by the sheet of wind issuing from the windway cutting against the upper lip. In properly voiced pipes little wind actually enters the pipe itself, so that a feather placed at the top of an open pipe is not blown away, but calmly settles down; but the air column, corresponding to the length of the pipe, being violently agitated, the metal or wood of the pipe vibrates also, and the result is a musical note. With the exact scientific explanation we are not here concerned, but may at once proceed to deal with

Faults in the Speech of Pipes.

IF a small pipe is dumb, it will probably be through dust choking the windway. Use a soft pencil brush, and be chary of blowing small pipes with the mouth, because the moisture from the breath will also choke the windway and affect the speech. Reeds, of course, must on no account be tested in this way, as the result would be ruination through verdigris forming on the brass tongues.

Rattling noises accompanying the speech of a pipe may be traced to grit blowing about between the opening at the foot and the languid. If it will not drop out by shaking, or by inserting a wire through the foothole, this opening must be gently enlarged and beaten in again to its former size and shape, after which it must of course be again carefully regulated as to power to make it agree with those next it.   In a wooden pipe a tiny chip in the windway is often the cause of unsteady and imperfect speech; the cap may have to be taken off to remove it; the large pipes can have them screwed on, the smaller ones are glued.   A hissing noise accompanying a note will probably be caused by the foot of the pipe not fitting firmly into the hole on the upper-board.

Töpfer, in his monumental work on organ building, thus enumerates faults in the sound-producing parts of the flue pipes.

"A pipe may show in speaking the following defects :—

"(a) It will speak too late if the stream of wind goes too much outwards, or if the windway is too narrow.

"(b) It will fly off to the octave above if not cut high enough, or if the upper lip is bent outwards very much, or if the languid is too low, or the wind supply too strong through the windway being too wide.

"(c) It will yield a small, whizzing tone if the stream of wind meets the upper lip so that the proper tone cannot develop itself.   In this case, it may have too much wind, or the upper lip is bent inward too far, or the languid lies too high.

"(d) The pipes may be tremulous if they are not fixed firmly enough, or if the upper lip is bent outward too far, or if the windway is irregular, so that it is somewhat unequal in its width, or the windstream be unevenly directed.   The cause of tremulousness may also be found in too thin or imperfectly rounded pipes.

"(e) The pipes will sound feeble if the wind supply is inadequate,—that is, when the windway is too narrow.

"(f) They will yield a coarse tone if the wind-

way is too wide and also irregular, and the pipes
are at the same time too much cut up.

"(g) That pipes may differ in tone if some
sound so loud that they are ready to overblow.
Occasionally this defect is due to the pipes
being too thin, or unequal in thickness, or through
irregularities in the curvature of the lip, or in the
languid. The primary cause of this defect lies,
however, in the irregularity of wind from the
bellows."

"Speed" in Voicing.

PLAYERS are often dissatisfied with certain
stops without quite knowing the reason of
their discontent. The best way to develop
a keenness of ear in criticising tone quality
is to try the stops separately, just an octave at a
time and very slowly, weighing each note and
marking those which give the quality of tone
desired throughout the whole stop. Mere loudening or softening is a simple matter, but there are
other factors affecting pipe speech, and one of the
most important of these is its *relative speed*. In
badly voiced organs, we shall probably find certain
stops hard and unsympathetic throughout, instead
of yielding a flood of rich and mellow foundation
tone. It seems to the inexperienced that a stop
cannot be too quick in speaking ; but some stops
(notably the open diapason and the dulciana) are
purposely voiced so that they shall not be too
"prompt" in speech, because considerable richness
and character is imparted to the tone by letting it

settle down to the true note, breathing it out, so to speak, instead of blurting it out with a hard percussive effect.

This difference between prompt attack and slow speech must of course be very slight, and cannot be expressed in seconds or any fractional time measurement, but is rather the expression of the voicer's instinct as to the quality of tone the pipe may be made to give. And the whole stop must conform to it, since nothing is more offensive in regulation than great variation in the degrees of promptness; it is detected at once when the stop is used alone in a scale passage. This little secret of the voicer's art, though a commonplace to experienced voicers, is difficult for amateurs to realise until they have not merely played, but critically and slowly examined, stop by stop, many organs of different types, one with another, in the manner indicated.

If, for instance, a note in an open diapason stand out from the rest, is sharper and clearer in chords, yet not louder, it is said to be "too quick," and the remedy lies in slightly pressing in the upper lip, quite evenly, with some flat tool of suitable width, such as a chisel. If the reader has the patience to test as suggested all the dulcianas, for example, in a number of different organs, he will appreciate this point, upon which I have laid so much stress. But before dealing with the metal pipes, it will be best to turn the foregoing information into practice with respect to the wooden pipes.

Regulation of Stopped Wood Pipes.

WE will suppose an improvement is desired in some very unsatisfactory bass octave. The regulation may have been hurriedly done in the beginning (for many organs, even when built of good materials, have been put up in a hurry, some stops never receiving a final regulation in position), or the pipes may have got out of regulation through many years of neglect or ill usage.

In trying over an octave, slowly and critically, CC (let us suppose) is much louder than the rest ; CC♯ has an unpleasant escape of wind with the note ; DD is scarcely audible ; DD♯ comes on with an unpleasant " coughing " or " chipping " sound before settling down to its true note ; EE is the most musical note of the octave ; FF sounds a decided harmonic, spoiling the true note ; FF♯ has a rattling sound ; GG is particularly poor in quality ; GG♯ throbs like a tremulant ; and so on.

EE, being our best note, we must try to make the others exactly like it in power and quality. Soften CC, and any other pipe which is merely too loud, by inserting some more plugging (soft deal) into the foot until it is of the same degree of power as our best note. CC♯ has perhaps a badly fitted pipe-foot, which needs rasping or glass-papering to adapt it to the hole in the upper-board, so that no wind escapes before reaching the pipe ; or perhaps the foot may be split. Examine also the stopper, to see if it is loose and needs "packing" with a layer of paper inside the white leather surrounding its sides. Or the cap may need readjusting, some wind escaping between it and the block ; or the pipe may be split at the top, the stopper helping to force the crack slightly open. If so, remove the stopper, run in some thin glue and screw together. All wooden stopped pipes should be either screwed together at the sides or have a stout tape glued around them to resist the pressure of the stopper ; it is not sufficient merely to glue and nail the sides. The stopper may have been pressed down at an angle, whereas it is essential to good speech that it should be horizontal. Before replacing the stopper, apply a little grease to the sides if they are dry, so that it may be perfectly airtight, yet move easily. A chisel-mark usually shows which end of the stopper corresponds with the front of the pipe.

In regulating, no attention is paid to the pitch ; uniformity of tone being first aimed at. Therefore, in replacing the stopper, leave it flat for the present. One should be able later to put it into tune with a firm pressure instead of being obliged to knock it down with a hammer, for the vibrations thus set up may disturb some of the smaller pipes.

DD may have its windway partly choked. Unscrew the cap and examine, if it cannot be cleared with a piece of card or a thin strip of soft wood. Or the cause may be simpler still. Perhaps the pipe has been so placed that the mouth has practically no speaking room. If it cannot be turned, the foot-hole may be plugged up and a new one bored with brace and bit in another position.

If the DD♯ will bear softening, more plugging at the foot will probably remove or modify the "cough" which ushers in the note ; otherwise the remedy is to cut away a little of the upper lip, taking care to leave the edge quite even ; not more than one-sixteenth of an inch at a time. But if, at proper pitch, the stopper is quite at the top of the pipe, it will be too short to allow of this. A "chipping" sound accompanying the note may be due to the nicking on the block being too shallow.

Examine FF for an open joint, screw or nail hole, which may affect the pipe by bringing some harmonic into prominence. (This effect of a hole in a stopped pipe has been turned to account for a special stop, and stopped harmonic pipes have occasionally been made.)* Large wooden pipes are not injured in tone by "staying" something against them; but in alterations and rebuildings, when screws are removed, the holes, if they have gone through, should be plugged.

The fault in the FF♯ may be chips of wood rattling about in the foot, or between cap and block, or something loose near the mouth of the pipe set in motion by the wind that issues from it. It should rarely be necessary to take off a glued cap.

Probably in GG the various parts are not accurately adjusted: compare its finish with that of the better notes, and see if one or more of the above faults is also a contributory cause.

GG♯ may throb in consequence of the wood being too thin to stand the vibration, or sympathy may be set up with some adjacent pipe through the mouths being too close. The remedies are easy once the cause of the fault is determined.

Unsteady tone, when caused by the pipes being too thin to bear the wind pressure, may often be cured by binding and glueing wide pieces of stout

---

* A small hole about the middle of stopped pipes causes them to overblow to the twelfth, their first upper partial. The trebles of the German flute (Snetzler, King's Lynn), the harmonic gedact (Norman & Beard, St. Catherine's College, Cambridge), and the zauberflöte (Michell & Thynne, Tewkesbury Abbey) are so treated.

tape around the centre of the pipe, or thick brown paper may be glued around the smaller pipes. Sometimes a thin wedge of wood pushed into the centre of the windway will steady the note. The defect here being due to overblowing, one would naturally see first if the pipe will bear a little more plugging at the foot without making it too soft.

Open Wood Pipes.

L ARGE wood open pipes should have for tuning purposes a sliding piece of wood held at the sides through slots cut in them. This is better than a single screw through a piece of wood partly covering a V-shaped opening. When they have been cut too short, pieces of wood have to be screwed over the top to flatten, thereby weakening the note. They must be firmly screwed or they will jar with the vibration of the pipe. Small open wood pipes have a saw-cut at the top, at the back of the pipe, in which is inserted a metal cover to serve as a lid to flatten or sharpen; or, preferably, the metal is rolled up, and then the pipes are less likely to be put out of tune by an accidental touch. Often in modern work metal feet are used instead of wood for the smaller pipes, it being considered more convenient to enlarge or reduce the whole than to use plugging. For the latter purpose, there is a very useful tool, though made for a different purpose,—a small pair of scissors for gripping the A string of the violin;

small pieces of plugging can be extracted by it without any danger of pushing them further into the pipe. Builders generally use a flat screw-driver.

Ears and Beards.

EARS and beards steady and intensify the tone, and are of special value when applied to small scale basses. They should be of hard wood, about one inch deep at CCC, and of similar thickness to the sides of the pipes, the ears extending as far as the splay of the upper lip, and the beard level with the upper edge of the cap. They flatten the pitch, and are therefore a remedy for pipes cut too short, as is sometimes the case in old organs.

Bourdons are sometimes met with having the cap projecting high above the block, a fault in construction giving impure notes in which the fifth predominates. Large scale bourdons with the square block, well made and suitably placed, should be capable of yielding pure musical notes; and the same care ought to be taken to secure a perfectly even regulation in the pedal stops as in those of the manuals. But, if other means fail, the blocks should be re-made after the German model, which gives a full and satisfactory tone to even small pipes.   The two forms are shown in the accompanying sketch :—

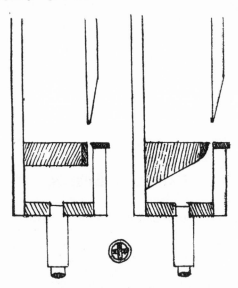

Fig. 1.

The blocks are faced in front with mahogany, also the tops of the caps forming the beard.   They are not always nicked, but nicking is considered to help the blending properties of pipes.   Too deep nicking, however, is one of the causes of windiness.   The method of inserting the plugging (end-grain pieces of soft deal) is also shown in the sketch.   The sound-board holes into which the pipe feet enter should be leathered to prevent any wind escaping, when the ends of the pipe feet are not tapered.

The Regulation of Metal Pipes.

A METAL pipe is loudened by inserting a penknife at the foot, and in passing it round, paring off a little of the metal, thus enlarging the hole. It is softened by beating the hole slightly smaller with the flat part of a chisel. In the case of small pipes a very minute alteration is usually sufficient, and the enlargement or compression of the hole may be effected with the tuning cone. A tendency to overblow or speak the octave is corrected by softening. Or the languid may be too low. In this case the two corners are slightly raised by inserting a piece of iron wire through the foothole. Or the mouth may be too low, when a slight paring of the upper lip with a sharp penknife is the remedy. The upper lip may be too convex, then press it in with the flat part of a chisel. Or the lower lip may be too concave; it is then drawn out evenly with a thin piece of metal. We must be very careful not to bruise the fine nicking when dealing with the mouth, or the pipe may refuse to speak at all. If it is necessary to open out the windway, use a thin piece of smooth hard wood; certainly not a penknife.

Much may be learnt by taking out the nearest pipe which speaks a good note and minutely comparing its mouth with that of the faulty pipe.

Slowness of speech, through the languid being too high, is cured by slightly pressing it down with the flat part of a chisel. But it may lie in the set of the upper lip, and that should be examined first. Or the lower lip being too convex, may need pressing in a little. Or it may be necessary to open out the windway a little.

Windiness may be traced to an irregular or too open windway or a bruised mouth ; sometimes to too deep nicking. If a whole set of pipes shows this defect, it is possible that the pipe feet may be too short.

In open pipes speaking over grooved wind, the purity of the note may be marred by a windy or hissing noise. Provided there is no actual wind escape to account for this and the pipe is firm in its hole on the sound-board, a cure may often be effected by slightly closing in the windway and, by way of compensation for this softening of the pipe, opening the foothole. Very long feet will sometimes produce or magnify this unpleasant defect. Every pipe should be expected to yield a firm, clear note of musical quality.

It is a common fault in small and cheap organs to place a flat of open diapasons just above the player's head, in a straight line with the case, whereas a slightly overhanging front is desirable, as the slight "hiss" heard at too close quarters from the prospect pipes will then pass over the player's head. The over-hang should not exceed two feet or the music desk will be darkened too much, and the player will be liable to underestimate the volume of tone he is using to accompany.

Hollow tone as the result of an overcut lip means re-making the pipe, removing the foot and lowering the top a little, an operation for the pipe maker. If the lips have been cut up too high, the wind will not "reach."

If much work has to be done, a steel tapered point to louden small pipes should be obtained from one of the supply houses ; also a "knocking-up" cup to soften. This has a much flatter taper, to avoid putting the foot out of shape.

Treatment of String Toned Stops.

GAMBAS and viols furnished with ears and beards, and speaking more or less in a strained or artificial register, are the most difficult to treat, for the smaller pipes especially are so easily spoilt by a false touch.

Slowness or unsteadiness of speech are the principal defects and one must experiment very cautiously indeed if the work has to be done in the organ itself. Examine first for dust or grit and brush out the windway gently with a fine camel hair brush. If on replacing, the speech is no better, examine the set of the little roller or frein in front of the mouth. Frequently, a slight turn of this will effect the desired cure. Slowness of speech is more or less inherent with small scale viol basses. The older types of string toned stops, tuned by long ears, are the tuner's *bêtes noirs*; little can be done to turn these into satisfactory stops, and they are best consigned to the melting pot and replaced with good modern stops from the pipe maker.

Treatment of Reeds.

THIS is the most exacting part of the voicer's work. It is the supreme test of his patience and fine eye for curves. It demands a fine ear, trained by experience gained through constant comparison of the reed work of various voicers, good, bad, and indifferent. To re-voice an entire reed stop in the organ itself would be a very long and tedious undertaking, as one pipe might have to go in and out of its place a dozen or more times before even a tolerably good note was obtained, and so the usual advice given to amateurs in works on the organ with regard to the regulation of reeds is similar to *Mr. Punch's* famous advice "to those about to marry." It is certainly safe, but not helpful. Since many are cut off from practical help and many tuners have but a limited knowledge of reed voicing, the hints here given may, at any rate, help the reader to improve a few exceptionally bad notes that worry him. And although a reed is more easily upset than any other pipe, the risk of irretrievable damage is not so great as in the attempts to re-voice small flue pipes. A tongue must indeed be in a hopeless condition if reburnishing and careful curving effects no improvement, and a few spare tongues can be obtained to experiment with.

The manner of removing and cleaning has been already described. After cleaning, see that in replacing the shallot its flat edge is perfectly parallel with the straight edge of the block. There should be a notch in the brass showing how far it enters. If too easily pushed beyond this, a piece of stout paper underneath the small end, opposite the side which receives the wedge, will keep it in place.

The broad end of the tongue must be strictly parallel to the broad flat edge of the reed or shallot, else the note will certainly be a bad one. The tuning wire must bear quite evenly upon the tongue, moving up and down freely, yet not too loose. If very hard to move, it may draw the tongue out of the wedge when knocked down to sharpen; if too loose, the vibrating of the tongue itself or a slight accidental touch will put the pipe out of tune.

Mr. Alfred Palmer, a well known pipe maker,

gives the following plain instructions for placing a reed stop on the sound-board:—

"1. On receiving the pipes take great care that no particle of dust or grit gets to them.

"2. Frequently move the drawstops in and out whilst holding down the keys when the wind is in.

"3. Well brush out sound-board holes with a feather or bottle brush.

"4. Put each reed boot in its place and pass the wind through, after which put the pipes or speaking parts in their places.

"5. If when tuning a pipe it becomes too soft as the result of being too flat, lower the pitch of the note by the spring, and reduce the length of the pipe in proportion by cutting down at top. If the stop is an oboe or clarinet with caps, the cap may be opened or closed as required, instead of cutting. Or, in the case of stops having regulating tongues (see next rule), the tongue can be similarly opened or closed.

"6. The regulating tongues usually found near the tops of the basses of stops of the trumpet family are not intended to be opened very wide or rolled, but opened from one fifth to half an inch. If more than this is required, the pipe is too long.

"7. If the tone of a pipe suffers from having dust or grit in it, as it often does, first pull the spring close down to the wedge, and then carefully clean the reed by passing a thin piece of writing paper between the tongue and the reed, gently pressing on the tongue. Care should be taken that the offending substance is not merely pushed further under the tail of the tongue instead of being expelled.

"8. Never attempt to tune a reed affected by dust, &c., but rather clean it first as described in the previous rule; otherwise the spring, riding over the intruding matter, may ruin the tongue.

"9. Never place a reed pipe to the mouth and blow it."

From the foregoing advice it will be seen that the inexperienced should not hastily meddle with reed stops. But those who cannot command the frequent services of a tuner should at least understand the tuning and cleaning.

Consonance of the Tube.

REEDS are mostly more or less faithful representations of the orchestral instruments whose names they bear, and the particular *timbre* of each is chiefly due to the shape of the tube. If, for example, by way of experiment, we interchange the shallot and tongues of an oboe and clarinet pipe, the pipe itself would still determine the general character or quality of the note. The trumpet, horn and cornopean, open at the top, have slots for regulating their power; the oboe and contra fagotto are capped and sometimes slotted as well; the straight tubes of the clarinet or corno di bassetto and vox humana are provided with slides. With these aids the tube is brought into sympathy or consonance with the true note of the tongue; when it is "out of period" it will fly off its speech.

As in flue pipes, a full, weighty tone is best obtained from thick, plain metal tubes of generous scale, and from spotted metal when we desire a brighter and more ringing quality. Spreading out the tube, trumpet fashion, naturally makes for power; whilst the narrow, straight tubes of clarinet and vox humana, by partially strangling the

tone, give us the more artificial quality of tone we
associate with those stops; and the orchestral
oboe, being of narrower scale than the more commonly used type of oboe, yields a more characteristic and piercing quality of tone.

Tubes which are too thin, producing a tone
which is both thin and harsh, as in so many old
organs, may be to a considerable extent improved
by fitting rings of leather or felt, with the edges
neatly joined and the size of each gauged so that
it will fit nicely about the centre of the tube. The
experiment may be tried by selecting some especially harsh note in a trumpet or horn stop.

Tubes of half length are often used for economy and where height is sadly lacking; but the
tone naturally cannot be so full and foundational,
the ground note not being there to give body to
the tone. A really fine chorus reed, with its full
length tube well in consonance, gives one almost
the impression of a soft stopped diapason humming along with it. In the strict attention to this
point, and to an exceedingly fine ear in regulating,
lay the secret of the exquisite purity and firmness
of tone of the late Mr. Henry Willis's reed work;
and there was a period in Victorian times when it
was absolutely unapproached by any other English
builder, by none in Germany, and possibly only
by Cavaillé-Coll in France. Now-a-days, if it is
not strictly true that "All may grow the flower, for
all have got the seed," good reed voicing is no
longer confined to one or two firms. The supreme
test is that every reed should be quite satisfactory,
even when used alone in chords creating its
own ground tones sufficiently to that end.

In the commonplace "commercial" organ, so
long as the reeds come into tune and are approximately of the same quality, they are passed; and
the organist is some day annoyed with a note
or two flying quite off its speech—possibly with

dirt on the tongue — but just as probably through the tube being too far out of period with the vibration set up by the tongue to allow for any further variations in the length of the tongue, such as the tunings at various periods of the year render necessary. There is a certain latitude within which the tongue compels the sympathetic vibration of the tube; and here is a matter for the student of acoustics to investigate and tell us, in a set of pipes of given scale and pitch, what the limits precisely are, from the lowest to the highest pipe; then, if we were enabled to adjust our reeds right into the centre of these boundaries, we should get a more scientifically accurate agreement which great extremes of heat and cold could scarcely upset.

When the tube is out of period with the tongue, the note flies off to some harmonic, usually a fifth, when being brought into tune, when cap, slide or slot must be adjusted and the note thoroughly tested at the key-board until this tendency is no longer observed.

Bearing in mind, then, the influence exerted by the tube, some defects to which the tongue is liable may be enumerated.

1. A note which is too weak, yet at the same time very prompt in speech, will have its tongue set too close to the reed,—insufficiently curved. If the brass is too soft, the mere riding up and down of the spring may have lessened the original curve, so that the stop will not stand well in regulation. Travelling tuners, desiring to improve a note of this kind, usually rely on the use of a penknife. The wire being drawn back, the blade of the knife is passed under the tongue and the curve is slightly widened; but if the sweep of the curve itself is altered in outline in the least degree the result will be a bad note. A reed block and a

burnisher are necessary if we wish to do good work. The great difficulty in obtaining a curve which will yield a good note lies in this: with the tuning wire hard up against the wedge, and drawing the finger in its stead along the tongue until it reaches the broad end, the tongue must be flat and even for its whole length along the reed. If on holding it up to the light, any light is seen between the tongue and the reed we may be certain that the result will be a poor note, for the whole under surface of the tongue cannot in that case beat evenly against its shallot. The faintest resemblance to the letter "S" in the curvature is fatal to good tone, as is also the slightest twist or buckling on one side.

2. A note may be too slow when first touched, yet repeat quickly. The slowness is due to too wide a curve; the quick repetition is accounted for by the fact that the tongue being still in a state of vibration is easily made to repeat its note, though when perfectly still it may be slow to start. Half a minute must therefore elapse before touching again, when testing for slowness. Slowness means power; for, tongue and reed being wider apart, the amplitude of vibration is increased. The curve must be lessened until it conforms to the adjacent note as to relative speed, as in the case of the flue stops already dealt with.

3. A note of bad quality may be caused by a minute indentation or twist of the tongue almost needing a microscope to detect. A badly injured tongue must be replaced by another of exactly the same thickness and curvature.

To obtain a round full volume of tone the voicer endeavours to make the curvature of the tongue as wide as he can without developing slowness of speech, and the higher the wind-pressure the easier his task becomes. For this reason also reeds are placed whenever practicable directly over the pallets, so that they may have the benefit of the first sudden inrush of wind.

Large reeds often have the edges against which the tongue beats covered with leather to soften them, but the best voicers obtain the quality they seek without this makeshift. More legitimate is the device, in order to prevent rattling by slowing down the beats, of weighting the end of the tongue by soldering on a piece of metal in the case of large pipes, or a piece of thick felt in the smaller ones. A whole stop is often treated in this fashion with good results, and thin tongues are often thus made to yield good notes. In fitting new tongues, the voicer usually begins by discovering experimentally how thick he may have them on the given wind pressure and then what diminutions in the thickness become necessary as the scale ascends.

The voicer's reed block is usually a smoothly planed surface of steel about a foot in length, with a steel clamp at one end for holding down the narrow end of the tongue ; and the burnisher is a curved piece of smooth steel attached to two wooden handles. A spare shallot, if straight, makes a tolerable substitute. But the practice of certain travelling tuners of filing an unsatisfactory tongue to "improve" it must be severely condemned. Should it become absolutely necessary to thin a tongue, it should be rubbed quite evenly upon the block over a piece of the finest (No. 0) glasspaper, worn down so that no scratches are visible on the brass. A magnifying glass may assist a beginner in this and in studying curves, but those who are continually at this branch of organ building develop a kind of instinct for the right curvature of the tongues, making a whole set with but very little subsequent touching over. Machinery has also been brought into use to assist.

The amateur who perseveres in improving a few
exceptionally bad notes which trouble him will,
at any rate, realise the desirability of being very
particular from whom he obtains new reed stops,
or into whose hands he entrusts any wholesale
re-voicing of his reed work.

The English Diapason.

THE great organ diapason is the most important and representative stop of the
whole organ, but ideals have differed
greatly as to the character of tone it
should possess. Three distinct types, however,
stand out prominently.

The English diapason may be recognised at
its best in good specimens by such typically English builders as Walker, Hill, or Bishop. The
mouths are mostly one quarter the circumference
of the pipe, and the best results have been obtained from good thick plain metal, the voicer
aiming at weight and fulness of tone with just
enough of the upper partials in evidence to give
a little "life" to it; the scale at CC being from
five to six inches.

The thin, old-fashioned type of English diapason, on the light wind-pressures of a century ago,
sounds relatively almost like a dulciana by the
side of the best modern specimens, and is therefore
quite unsuited to our present-day great or swell
manuals. It is nearly always a mistake to attempt
to get a greater power from them; loudening
usually takes all the "bloom" off the tone and
ruins them altogether. When worth retaining, it
is much better to relegate them to a light choir

organ on their original pressure (probably about 2½in.).

Mr. T. C. Lewis thus defined his ideal diapason tone, preferring spotted metal to give the desired brightness of tone :—

" My standard of an ideal diapason tone, as for a representative organ of good size, may be stated as the tone given by a cylindrical pipe, called two foot C, which is $2\frac{3}{16}$in. in diameter, having a mouth in width one quarter of the circumference, and its height $\frac{3}{8}$ and $\frac{3}{32}$ of an inch ; at the foot, a windhole $\frac{3}{8}$in. and $\frac{1}{16}$in. in diameter, the wind pressure by gauge $3\frac{1}{2}$ in., the pitch $267\frac{1}{2}$ vibrations at 60 deg. Fahrenheit ; the pipe being voiced to sound its note firmly, yet leaving it securely within that verge, beyond which it might fly off to its octave."

It may be remarked that even with such minute directions for fixing a standard, the precise thickness and weight of metal, also the boldness or fineness of the nicking, are very important factors leaving a margin for considerable differences in tone.

The German Type.

THIS quality of tone is found at its best in some remarkably fine specimens of the work of Edmund Schulze, of Paulinzelle, in his organs at Armley, Tyne Dock, Hindley, Wigan and Doncaster. It is obtained from a wider mouth ($\frac{2}{7}$in.) with a more copious supply of wind through a large foot-hole, a bold ringing tone being aimed at, of a character very grand and telling in lofty churches of good acoustic qualities. This type has influenced considerably

the work of some of our English builders, such as
Lewis and Binns, but in a modified form as considered by them more suitable to ordinary English
churches.   There exist some fine specimens in
wood ; but as they give the voicer more trouble,
and the metal foundation is required for the front
pipes, examples in wood can never become general.
The reason why firm clear notes, even throughout
the scale, are not so readily obtained from wood
diapasons will be apparent when one considers
that the upper lip and languid are not so amen-
able to treatment as in the metal pipe; and pedal
opens which are windy, irregular and less musical
in the upper part than pipes of the same pitch on
a good metal open 8ft., are all too common.

The Diapason with Leathered Lip.

A N upper lip, when covered with leather,
has the effect of reducing the hardness or
brilliance of tone, just as a soft hammer
striking a piano string will produce a
softer and more muffled tone.   The aim in each
case is to obtain more foundation tone through
suppressing the upper partials.   To compensate
for the loss of power in the organ pipe, the foot-
hole is enlarged.   If we reduce the diapason to the
level of a dull flute, we create a gap between it
and the upper work, to the detriment of the building up of tone to the full organ.   But cases may
be cited where harsh, overcut and overblown
diapasons have been entirely transformed into
good stops by leathering the upper lip.   If over-
done, the result is a weak, fluffy tone, and only
actual experiment can decide.   The device was

largely exploited by the late Robert Hope-Jones, and there are many specimens in organs bearing his name, with a smooth, rolling tone of fine quality, on high wind pressures.

If we find a hard and coarse-toned diapason as the result of an attempt to louden an unsatisfactory set of pipes, the experiment is well worth trying, as it may be so easily done without permanent injury to the stop. Some scraps of bookbinders' leather being procured, it would be well first to test the four notes of a chord in the middle of the keyboard,—say C, E, G, C. The leather is put on with seccotine, about half-an-inch inside the upper lip and an inch outside. The effect of course would be to flatten the pitch, which must be adjusted by slides, and if necessary by slightly paring a little off the top. The wind-hole must be enlarged to regain the power lost. Thinner leather, bookbinders' cloth or cartridge paper may be best for the upper octaves; or, to preserve the crescendo in the extreme treble, it may be desirable to do without. It should be noted that if the wind pressure is a relatively low one for the building, disappointment is likely to follow experiments in this direction.

Although the leather has sometimes been applied to the upper lip of wood pipes, I have not found it improve the tone of old ones, the upper lip being usually thick enough.

The whole problem is one of overtones,—what suggestion of the octave or other intervals the voicer chooses to permit along with the ground note. If he excludes all brightness and ring, he creates a ponderous dull flute or a weak characterless tone, according to the nature of his material. The opposite extreme is pronounced hard and lacking in foundation tone; thus great scope exists for individuality of treatment and the study of tone colour becomes a fascinating one. For the ear can certainly be educated to detect an overtone, more especially the octave, sounding simultaneously with the ground note. The illusion is sometimes so marked that one thinks another pipe is actually speaking.

The Violin Diapason.

THIS is the equivalent of the geigen principal in German specifications. The quality of tone is obtained by slightly reducing the scale and allowing the upper partials to give the pipes a little of the string quality. As with all the gamba class, spotted metal helps. It is better suited to the swell than to the weighty foundation tone we expect on the great, which often sounds rather dull when boxed. As the tendency of the box is to thin down harmonics, it may easily happen that an open, which is too bright and hard on an open sound-board, will be quite transformed by enclosure.

Horn diapason, harmonic open and bell diapason represent less desirable varieties of foundation tone, and the gemshorn is seldom made at 8ft. pitch.

Slotted Diapasons.

THE effect of cutting slots in an open diapason is to create a hybrid quality of tone akin to the gamba. The practice is universal with French builders, the French montre having a tone quality which is most unsatisfying to English ears. The late Mr. Henry Willis usually treated his diapasons in this way with the object of getting a better tonal scheme, through the fusion of the overtones thus created. He relied on the exquisite purity of his reed work to give a satisfactory balance to the full organ, together with extreme keenness of ear and patience in the regulation of each individual stop. Yet it is indisputable that real diapason tone ought to predominate, and the effect of full organ up to mixtures should be at once rich, dignified and brilliant, without the ear craving the addition of reeds to satisfy it. Ideals and standards of taste change, but it would seem at present that slotting should be confined to the stops which are intended to be keen and "stringy." As slides are not practicable for front pipes, these are provided with a wide slot near the top for tuning.

In converting a slotted diapason, it will often be necessary to shift the pipes up one or two notes from tenor C when cutting down the top for slides. Even if we are unable to cut away the slotted part entirely, the tone is not impaired provided the top of the slide is level, overlapping a little.

Octave Stops.

THE name "principal"—given in German organs to the diapasons, because they are the most important stops in every organ— is applied in English instruments to the chief 4ft. stop, because that is the stop by which all the others are tuned. It is made one pipe smaller in scale than the open diapason at 4ft. pitch. Standing in the centre of the tone-mass—

clear, bright and incisive, though too "hard" to use alone — its function is to impart brilliance to the more mellow foundation work; and spotted metal gives the best results. In small organs the gemshorn is often preferred as the swell 4ft. stop, in the interests of variety. The true gemshorn is of conical shaped pipes, this favouring an agreeable reediness; and in artistically voiced organs certain combinations become effective, which would not be so with the more brilliant principal. On the choir organ, the first 4ft. stop to be included is usually a flute,—wald flute, lieblich flute, or suabe flute. A gemshorn is useful in many ways, when we are able to extend our choir organ to seven or eight stops. But here, in three manual organs, the claims of the "combined solo and choir" step in, and the gemshorn is not often found in addition to a 4ft. flute, except in quite large instruments. A small scale stopped flute, unless all the other stops are very carefully treated, is apt to give a nasal quality in combination.

Flute Tone.

FLUTE tone may be divided into two classes,—open and stopped. The most usual varieties of open flute are the clarabella, wald flute, höhl flute and harmonic flute. The clarabella, of wood, large in scale, and with an inverted mouth, usually has a stopped bass. Bolder in tone, and valuable as a solo stop, it has replaced the stopped diapason on the great manual in modern English organ building. Although giving more body of tone, it rarely blends well with the dulciana, which it overpowers in small organs. The wald flute as found at 8ft. pitch in Messrs. Walker's organs, with the mouth on the narrow side of the pipe, usually blends better, and is of somewhat different tone quality, being sweet and cloying. Backed by a good oboe (with the shutters closed), it gives the nearest resemblance to the orchestral horn. At 4ft. pitch, it is one of the best choir organ flutes. The höhl flute, met with in both triangular and rectangular form, is frequently preferred in the specifications of Messrs. Hill, Binns and others. It has less body, a hollow, liquid quality of tone being aimed at. The tibia plena of the Hope-Jones organs is, practically, a very large scale (9in. at CC) clarabella, more liquid, and yet at the same time more powerful than any of the other open flutes, requiring a high wind pressure and a sound-board extended to about 11ft. to do it justice. A good specimen is valuable on a solo organ; but large scale flute stops have a disturbing influence, as a rule, in ordinary instruments, generating much sympathy. As to large scale clarabellas, I have found, by actual experiment, the same stop, voiced for $2\frac{5}{8}$in. pressure, sound like a totally different stop on 4in., and again on 5in. pressure, each time gaining both in power and liquidity of tone; whilst all the other stops subjected to the increase were rendered coarser and would have needed much re-voicing to adapt them to it. The harmonic flute of 8ft. pitch is more in evidence in French organs than in English, where it is usually chosen as the 4ft. great flute. Cavaillé-Coll is credited with the discovery that, by employing metal flutes of double length for the trebles and piercing the body of the pipe with a small hole, a distinctly clear and liquid quality of tone could be produced. This small hole is usually about $\frac{2}{8}$ths up from the mouth of the pipe. As a choir 4ft. stop, it is called flauto traverso by some builders.

The chief stopped varieties are the old English stopped diapason (invariably of wood), and the smaller scale lieblich gedact, with a higher mouth, a little brighter tone, and a decided "chip" accompanying the speech of the pipe. It is either of wood or metal, was introduced into England by Schulze and very successfully copied by the late Mr. T. Lewis, in some of whose choir organs a family of gedacts may be found at 16ft., 8ft. and 4ft. pitch. By perforating a long stopper in old organs by a sliding cap and "chimney," we obtain the somewhat more open variety of tone usually named rohr flöte (reed flute), which does not, as is sometimes erroneously stated, refer to the quality of tone we associate with reed stops, but to the species of stopper. The cor de nuit on modern choir organs is a species of quintatön. By large scales and a low mouth the voicer develops the twelfth upper partial, giving a piquancy to the ground note and blending well with other suitably voiced foundation stops.

I should like here to urge the retention of the English term, stopped diapason. Open diapason, stopped diapason: what more natural in an English organ? Well made, of large scale, and with inverted mouth, it can hold its own with the gedact, and on the great blends better with the dulciana than most open flutes ever do. The reason for putting the clarabella in its stead is not solely to "gain more body;" but, I suspect, because the extra amount of wood required for the trebles is less a consideration with the builder than the trouble of making so many small stoppers. The neat workmanship of many of the old English builders in this detail is worth noting,— and copying.

String Tone.

FROM the quiet dulciana and viol d'amour to the keen modern viol d'orchestre, this quality of tone, bringing the upper partials into more or less prominence along with the ground note, is effected by using smaller scales, a low cut and sharper mouth; and, to increase the amplitude of vibration, a bar or frein outside the lower lip, or the roller outside the mouth of viols, thus assisting the voicer's endeavours to make these more artificial tones speak promptly by checking the intake of air. Slotting also favours stringiness. As the names are generally used in English organs the varying degrees, from pp to f as to keenness and power, may be thus approximately given:—

1. Dulciana, sometimes bearded.
2. Salicional, a little fuller in tone, usually slotted.
3. Gamba, viol da gamba, or viola, keener in tone.
4. Viol d'orchestre, the smallest in scale of all 8ft. stops.

There is also a modification of this last, the muted viol, or viole sourdine, with tapering pipes; and good specimens have a distinct charm of their own. The echo gamba, viol d'amour, vox angelica, &c., are further attempts at refinement and delicacy from the first three classes.

It may be taken as a general rule that the keener the more characteristic and orchestral stops of the gamba class are voiced the less well do they blend with pure diapason tone; on the other hand, exceptionally rich combinations may be got from a keen string tone stop and a powerful and liquid flute tone by good modern voicers. These, however, are special effects which should not intrude upon the building up of a dignified great organ tone.

String toned stops, like reeds, are always at their best behind swell shutters. Ingenious attempts have been made by modern voicers to obtain a string quality of tone from a stopped metal bass, but it is naturally feeble in tone compared to an open bass.

VOIX CELESTES.

The effect of a string orchestra can be simulated to a remarkable degree by the class of stops we are considering. Beating ranks, applied to diapasons, reeds or flutes would be most offensive to the ear, although there is a type of small scaled stopped gedact or zauberflöte, occasionally met with and labelled unda maris, to which a slow beat is given. But the term is also applied to a céleste formed of two very delicately voiced ranks of dulciana pipes. On the sound-board it is best to interpose some other stop between the two string toned ranks, otherwise in tuning the sharper rank it may "draw" the other into tune with it, refusing to give a steady beat at the required pitch.

The ordinary céleste rank is another set of pipes, usually only to tenor C, of the gamba family, tuned a little sharper than the gamba, salicional or viol against which it beats. In many important modern organs there is a flat rank as well, thus avoiding the slight feeling of dulness, or flatness in pitch when the stop is pushed in. In tuning, the keener the quality of tone, the more pronounced the beats should be to produce a good effect. It is almost as much abused by amateurs as the tremulant, but, provided it is not inserted at the expense of some important foundation stop, it is of decided value in quite a small organ, in the interests of variety. As to its *raison d'être*, every musical reader is no doubt aware that the effect of a string quartet is totally different to that of an orchestra of strings, even when the latter is playing the same passage as softly. There is more "life" in the latter, though the tone is not so pure, and each part has lost its individuality. This is because of the slight variability of intonation existing in a number of players playing the same part, and the "wave" thus set up is imitated with considerable success by the slightly "out of tune" rank. All voix célestes effects must issue from a swell box to make their due effect, and a lower standard than good spotted metal should never be permitted except for the CC octave, which may be of zinc.

As an instance of the modern development of string tone, the solo organ of Ely Cathedral, as rebuilt by Messrs. Harrison of Durham is noteworthy. Five of the eleven stops provide a powerful and complete family group of this special timbre :—

1. Contra viola, 16ft.
2. Viole d'orchestre, 8ft.
3. Viole céleste, 8ft.
4. Viole octaviante, 4ft.
5. Cornet de violes (10, 12, 15).

Harmonic flute, 8ft., concert flute, 4ft., harmonic piccolo, 2ft., clarinet, 8ft., orchestral hautboy, 8ft., and tuba, 8ft., complete this interesting solo manual, all being in a swell box except the tuba. Octave, sub-octave, and unison - off couplers are also available.

Mixture Work.

I T may not be unprofitable to regard the work of the great organ as one large mixture expressed thus:—

16ft., 8ft., 8ft., 8ft. [8ft.], 4ft., 4ft., 2ft., 2¾ft.,

IV. rank mixture.

The principal 4ft., firm, bright and clear in tone, is the central point of the whole tonal structure, and much care in the choice of appropriate scales and relative degrees of power is necessary to secure a fine *ensemble*. It is a present day error to omit the twelfth from this scheme, since it gives a bell-like cohesion to the whole, and a still greater one to choose a "fancy" 2ft. stop, such as a piccolo or flautina, instead of a plain, honest fifteenth. Various kinds of fancy mixtures have been made: viol mixtures, lieblich mixtures, and dulciana mixtures, but these may be relegated to echo organs or exceptional chamber instruments. On that point I am enabled to quote from an interesting essay on mixtures received from Mr. Vincent Willis. The writer, Mr. A. F. Duprey,* has had considerable

* Being in the R.N.V.R., Mr. Duprey was engaged in patrol work, and his cruiser was torpedoed in December, 1917, in the Irish Channel. Mr. V. Willis writes: "Organ building loses a promising votary, and I lose a dear friend."

experience in England, France and Germany in organ construction. He says:—

"There is no necessity to fly to mixture stops whose ranks are composed of pipes of different tone colours. Such high-flown ideas are quite impracticable. In every species of stop the characteristic tone tends to disappear as the pipes get into the higher octaves. The smallest pipes of viols, salicionals, flutes and lieblich all differ in little but power from one another. The diapason pipe carries its characteristic quality in the smaller pipes higher than any other kind, and being a stop of the most stable intonation is undoubtedly the fittest to use for all classes of mixture work."

There exists some confusion in defining the term "mutation rank." Some writers include all the octaves above the prime tone, but it should only be applied to those ranks which sound notes other than those of the octaves of the key put down. The most important of these are the "fifth" sounding ranks, expressed by the figures 12, 19, 26. Next comes the tierce, or "third" sounding rank, starting with the 17th, and maintaining it nearly to the top. The flat 21st can only be tolerated in the very comprehensive mixture schemes of large organs, and the tierce is not so much in evidence as it used to be in the days of the old builders and their light wind pressures. The unison and octave sounding ranks are expressed thus; 1, 8, 15, 22, 29.

As these very shrill pipes in their upper octaves have but half-an-inch or so of "speaking" length it is not practicable to carry them through without breaking back at suitable intervals, usually between C and C♯, the designer's aim being to prevent any unpleasant gap being felt. In actual playing these breaks are sufficiently covered by the other stops.

With these explanations, the following schemes should be quite intelligible. The slides should be divided, with a stout pin running through them, which may be drawn out for convenience when regulating or tuning. They are here indicated by the Roman numerals:—

A Three-Rank Mixture. (*i*).

I.   17th to C above mid C; 1st, C♯ to top.
II.   19th to fiddle G; 12th, G♯ to top.
III. 22nd to mid C; 15th to top.

A Three-Rank Mixture. (*ii*).

I.   12th to fiddle G; 15th to mid C; 19th to C
       above mid C; 12th to top.
II.   19th to mid C; 12th to C above mid C; 8th
III. 22nd to mid C; 15th to top.   [to top.

A Three-Rank Mixture. (*iii*).

I.   15th to BB (12 pipes); 12th tenor C to B¹
      (24 pipes); 7th C² to top.
II.   19th to BB (12 pipes); 17th to B (12 pipes);
      15th to B¹ (12 pipes); 12th to top.
III. 22nd to B (24 pipes); 17th C² to top (12 pipes);
      15th to top.

A Four-Rank Mixture. (*i*). Robson.

I.   17th to C above mid C; 1st C♯ to top.
II.   19th to F (1st space treble clef); 15th to C
      (3rd space treble clef); 19th to C (4th
      space); 8th C♯ to top.
III. 22nd to F; 19th to C; 12th C♯ to top.
IV. 29th to F; 22nd to C; 15th to top.

A Four-Rank Mixture. (*ii*).

I.   19th to fiddle G; 15th to mid C; 12th to C (third space treble clef); 1st to top.

II. 22nd to fiddle G; 19th to mid C; 15th to C; 8th to top.

III. 26th to fiddle G; 22nd to mid C; 19th to C; 12th to top.

IV. 29th to fiddle G; 26th to mid C; 22nd to C; 15th to top.

Not much can be done in the way of softening any particular rank, for, paradoxical as it may appear, to soften is generally to spoil by making it offensively "flutey" in character; each rank must be brilliant and ringing to have a good effect in the full organ. If almost on the verge of overblowing, so much the better, for the tendency of most large sound-boards to "rob" when nearly all the stops are employed (and it is under such conditions that mixtures are used) will reduce that fault to a minimum. But as will be seen by analysing the above schemes, there is scope for much ingenuity in covering the returns and hiding the breaks so that they are not perceptible to the player unless he searches for them by testing the mixture alone in a scale passage. A wish has sometimes been expressed that the player might be allowed the option of choosing his own mutation ranks,—e.g., with or without tierce; or regulating their assertiveness by enclosing a number of ranks within a swell, instead of being tied down to a particular voicer's conception of the best balance between them and the under structure of foundation tone as represented by the 16ft., 8ft., 4ft., and 2ft. stops. Probably the idea will be developed in organs of the future.

In organs containing a great mixture of four ranks with the tierce (17th), the full effect is often harsh. Careful cleaning, regulating, and accurate

tuning may ameliorate this; but a really well proportioned mixture can be made not only to add
brilliance, but actually seem to increase the foundation tone when the flat 21st is added, thus repro-
ducing the whole of the natural harmonic series,
for a fuller explanation of which the reader is re-
ferred to any work on acoustics. But these ranks
must be well proportioned to each other as to
brilliance, the octave sounding ranks being the
brightest, the "fifth" sounding ranks (12th, 19th,
26th) next, and the 17th, flat 21st less prominent.
Using note values to convey the idea of relative
brightness, we may suggest it pictorially thus:—

Such was Cavaillé-Coll's practice, the large organ
in Notre-Dame containing one such mixture on
the great giving the 8ft. harmonics, another on
the bombarde giving the 16ft. harmonics.

But economy steps in: the four rank mixture is
cut down to three, the twelfth omitted, and the
result is too often an empty effect which needs the
8ft. reed to cover it to make it tolerable; whereas
the direction "full great to mixtures" should represent an effect at once dignified and brilliant, without any reeds or couplers. All the leading ranks
should have low cut mouths to obtain brilliance
by encouraging the development of the upper
partials, and the use of spotted metal helps.

Two rank mixtures are occasionally specified
in small organs, consisting of fifteenth and twelfth.
But these should always draw separately, because

the 2ft. stop is sometimes required in conjunction with a 16ft. or 8ft. stop, either of the stopped or open class, with which, in the upper two octaves, it forms a light and brilliant solo as a valuable alternative to a 4ft. solo flute.

The 19th rank has occasionally appeared as an octave twelfth under the name of larigot, the word originally denoting a species of flute. The name "mixture" is used in modern work to cover all mutation stops formerly differentiated under a variety of names,—sesquialtera, fourniture, cornet, cymbale, &c.

In taking out the mixtures of an old organ particular care should be observed to keep not only the CC and CC♯ sides separate, but the ranks and their breaks also. They should be wrapped in parcels distinctly marked, to avoid trouble when replacing, for the old builders did not stamp their metal pipes with clear lettering, but merely scratched the letters on the metal. Pipes also may have been exchanged here and there, or a whole set transposed; and the amateur who starts gaily to remove a quantity of such pipes may find he has to deal with a "mixture" in more senses than one, and waste much time in sorting them out.

The Material of Pipes.

WEIGHT of metal is intimately connected with the weight of tone; and, if we desire a very solid foundation tone, our large great open diapason should be made of thick, heavy plain metal, with specially hardened feet to withstand the weight.

Stopped metal pipes may just as well be in plain metal; for keen viols pure tin is best; for all the rest of the flue work from 4ft. up and for the gambas, spotted metal. Cavaillé-Coll used pure tin for his reeds, but in England even spotted metal is considered a luxury rather than a necessity for the reed work. Before the great war, the CC octave of a 6in. scale open diapason, unvoiced, cost about £11, as against £7 or £8 for the complete stop with zinc for the lowest twelve notes, from a good pipe maker; but, unfortunately, these prices have now (1920) to be doubled, with no prospect of an ultimate reduction to their pre-war figure. Nevertheless, in the interests of artistic organ building, we plead for the best, even if, in new work, many stops have to remain for some time prepared for only.

If, however, in a bad system of close competition, the desire for spotted metal is met by some builder with the resolve to use smaller scales and thinner sheets of metal, the result will be less satisfactory than if that builder's original standard of metal had been accepted, with its larger scales and greater weight.

Again, it is misleading to point to some well voiced hard rolled zinc bass as superior to someone else's metal bass, or as being all that could be desired, for the fact remains that the same excellent voicing would yield much finer results with a heavier and thicker metal.

Zinc is appraised according to its substance: B.W.G.17 meaning Birmingham wire gauge 17. For the 16ft. octave, it can be made to yield excellent results, and such costly and unnecessary extravagances as 32ft. fronts in pure tin are not likely to be repeated.

Manual Doubles.

MANUAL stops of 16ft. pitch, adding depth and richness to the tone mass (and, incidentally, providing the player with some charming varieties of tone colour when played an octave higher with a soft 8ft. stop) should always be smaller in scale and subordinate in power to the 8ft. foundation work on the same key-board. Otherwise the effect is too heavy and thick. If the mouth of a bourdon is kept low, the fifth sounding upper partial is brought into prominence; and this fact has been utilised in the quintatön 16ft., with the idea of binding the tone more closely to the upper work. The 16ft. open diapason is, of course, much more expensive than the bourdon, but helps to make a very dignified front in a lofty chancel. In the author's opinion, large "great" organs having two doubles, both the bourdon and the open diapason are desirable before the double reed. When the latter is included, it certainly needs the 4ft. clarion to balance it. In the days of indifferent reed voicing, a small scale bourdon was invariably the first choice for the swell double; but there is a general feeling amongst modern players that a good small scale soft contra hautboy or contra fagotto is to be preferred. On the choir organ, a 16ft. dulciana is a beautiful stop, but a luxury to be expected only in large instruments.

No matter how softly a manual double is voiced, its addition to the tone mass is at once felt; this, of course, being due to the fact that a stop has been drawn of different pitch to the others. The same pipes, transferred to 8ft. pitch and drawn with the stronger 8ft. foundation stops of its own manual, would probably add nothing appreciable to the ear in the way of power. Sometimes the gamba quality of tone is preferred for the double, and a contra viola or contra gamba appears in the swell of many Willis and other specifications, but it should always have its own proper open bass.

The Blending of Stops.

I N the choice of correct scales, the player must rely on the experience of pipe makers and voicers; for, beyond a few general observations, very little help can be given without knowing the special conditions. Buildings easily make or mar the voicer's efforts: in one church everything blends, in another the organist is much restricted as to satisfactory combinations and tone building, and a good voicer will know best as to the advisability of certain stops.

When conditions are favourable, certain results may be obtained synthetically. A keen small scaled 8ft. viol, combined with a soft and liquid 2ft. flautina, will give an excellent imitation of an orchestral oboe, at any rate for the two or three middle octaves of the key-board, beyond which they stand out separately, refusing to blend. A 2ft. gemshorn will give a very plaintive or slightly nasal colouring to a clarinet or corno di bassetto, and a 4ft. lieblich flute will also make this reed stop appear as though the player had drawn quite another distinctive solo stop. A strong toned 8ft. flute or stopped diapason in some organs will yield a piquant and bell-like effect in combination with the twelfth. Again, some swell mixtures can be drawn with good effect in light and sparkling passages with only a lieblich gedact for the foundation, yet being none the less effective in the "full swell." Such results — first, no doubt, discovered empirically—are noted by shrewd voicers for reproduction under similarly favourable conditions. We have here also the key to the explanation why some old organs, carefully enlarged and rebuilt from time to time, still possess certain points of superiority to many entirely new and mechanically more perfect instruments, in which the builders have made a more or less lucky guess at the building up of tone in the factory, circumstances not permitting them entirely to voice and regulate the whole in the position for which it is designed, or to change entire stops for others. Whatever charm may be found in an old organ does not lie, as is popularly supposed, in the mellowing of age. An organ stop is not in the least like a violin in this respect.

It must be remembered that in the building up of tone we must regard principal, fifteenth, twelfth and mixture as *extensions* of the 16ft. and 8ft. diapasons, and on the great organ the piccolo, flautina or flageolet would only mar the effect of the whole.

The Wind Pressure.

CONTROLLED either by weights on bellows or reservoirs, or by spiral springs at their sides; recorded by a glass wind gauge placed temporarily in one of the soundboard holes and measured in inches, the extreme limits of wind pressure are from 1 inch to 50. $2\frac{1}{2}$ to 3 inches may be regarded as an average low pressure; anything above 5 inches as high. For ordinary church organs of three manuals seldom will anything exceeding 5 or 6 inches be required. On account of the key resistance, 4 or $4\frac{1}{2}$ inches is about the limit for tracker work and also for hand blowing. Under normal acoustic conditions all the flue stops of ordinary organs can be made to yield their best results with a pressure not exceeding 4 or $4\frac{1}{2}$ inches. Reeds gain most in quality and promptness when voiced on the higher pressures, but if for any special reason it is desired to place a powerful solo reed on the same soundboard as a very delicate stop of the dulciana or echo salicional class these latter, by greatly reducing the foothole, and careful treatment of the upper lip and the windway may be restored to their original delicacy of speech, so that no expert could say whether the pipes were speaking on a 2 or 10 inch wind. With reeds, however, it is quite otherwise, and a voicer may congratulate himself if he has turned out a really satisfactory reed of any sort on less than 3 inches. The relative advantages and drawbacks of low and high pressures may be thus set out :—

LOW PRESSURE.

Easy blowing—light touch — good for choir organ—inferior reeds—lack of power.

HIGH PRESSURE.

Heavier strain on bellows and increased cost of blowing—heavier touch (if tracker)—finer reeds— necessary for solo organ—greater power.

The effect musically of raising the wind pressure an inch or so in an organ of which the tone is too light and thin for the building (assuming the metal pipes are of sufficient substance) will usually be as follows :—

The reeds will gain in clearness, promptness and power. Large scale stops of the clarabella type will become clearer and more liquid. Bourdon basses will become windy and probably "cough," needing much regulation by plugging at the foot. The mixtures and all small metal trebles will give trouble through overblowing, flying off into the octave ; delicate stops of the dulciana class will lose much of their tranquil charm and the diapasons become more powerful but perhaps coarse.   Each stop will have to be taken in hand separately and patiently regulated, a work occupying many days, or the general impression conveyed to many musical hearers will be that "the organ has been spoilt."   There was once a parson in the West of England who "improved" his organ by the simple expedient of adding some heavy stones to the bellows, also overburdening the touch with extra sub and super octave couplers.   He was somewhat hurt to find that neither organist nor blower shared his satisfaction at the result !

Pressures from 1 to 2 inches only apply to chamber and echo organs.   The abnormal one of 50 inches exists in the organ at Ocean Grove, New Jersey, where the tuba, inside a swell box of peculiar construction, fitted with "sound - trap" joints, may be reduced to a *pianissimo* soft enough to accompany a solo. But it may well be doubted, from what we know of musical conditions in American churches, whether such exaggerated means of expression will be always reserved for purely artistic purposes. The enormously powerful and brilliant tubas in the Alexandra Palace organ, in a hall seating 15,000, do not exceed twenty-five inches.

Scales.

BY "scale," we understand the diameter of a cylindrical pipe, and it is usual for that diameter to halve at the seventeenth note. Modern voicers introduce relatively larger trebles into their foundation work and aim at a gradual *crescendo* upwards. In many of the old German organs, the tenor part was often rich and full and the trebles relatively weak ; and one feels in playing Mendelssohn, Rheinberger and Merkel especially that they expected, whilst holding a full chord in the right hand in a *forte* passage on the great organ, an important melodic phrase for the left hand to stand out prominently with both hands on the same manual.

Owing to this fundamental difference in treatment of scales and voicing, the effect on a modern organ is quite different to that on the organs of their day, and really a different type of instrument has been created. The very large scale pedal opens and bourdons of some of our old English builders have no place in German organs, but their pedal stops were far more numerous.

The late Mr. T. C. Lewis gave as a well-proportioned scale for an open diapason the following, also the weight (which in this class of stop is of great importance). CC diameter 6in.; tenor C 3½in.; middle C 2⅓in.; 1ft. C 1¼in.; 6in. C ¾in.; weight in spotted metal throughout, 4 cwt. In plain metal, an open diapason from tenor C to A is estimated by Mr. Alfred Palmer at 3 qrs. For a second open, 5in. at CC is deemed sufficient. Other scales are :—

FLUE PIPES.

Principal—CC, 3in. to 3¼in.
Dulciana—CC, 3½in.
Gamba—CC, 3in.
Viol d'orchestre—CC, 1⅛in. to 2in.
Principal—CC, 3¼in.
Fifteenth—CC, 1¾in.
Stopped diapason (wood)—CC, 4in. by 3½in.
L. gedact, rohr flöte or stopped diapason (metal)—CC, 3in. to 3½in.
Suabe flute—CC, 2½in.
Harmonic flute—CC, 2¾in.
Clarabella—middle C (wood), 2in. by 1⅝in.

REEDS.

Horn or cornopean—CC (at top), 5in.; tenor C, 3¾in.
Trumpet—CC, 4in.
Closed horn—CC, 4in.; tenor C, 3⅛in.
Oboe—CC, 2¾in. to 3in.; tenor C (bell), 2½in.
Clarinet—CC, 1¾in. to 2in.
Vox humana—CC, 1½in. to 2in.
16ft. pedal reed—CCC, 9in.
32ft. pedal reed—CCCC, 16in.

The CC of the principal should be one pipe smaller than the tenor C of the open diapason ; the fifteenth one pipe smaller than the principal, and the mixture ranks are similarly reduced in scale. The aim, as we ascend, being increased brightness but less power. Organs exist in which this well-tried rule has been disregarded and their "building up" of tone is harsh and disagreeable. In such cases, the only remedy (if the pipes are worth preserving) is to re-arrange and re-voice the whole of the upper work. The chief open diapason, principal, fifteenth, twelfth, and mixture are the backbone of the full organ and should be brilliant and ringing, somewhat over-brilliant, no doubt, without the enriching influences of the other stops. Some builders make their second great open diapason an exact replica as to tone quality of the first, but of less power,—and if gradations of tone were our sole consideration this is the best way to secure it ; but in the interests of variety a different type may well be inserted, avoiding of course any pronounced gamba tone, which does not blend well with real diapasons, although it fits well into the more flutey "montres" of French organs.

Those who have had much to do with chamber organs soon discovered that a few large scale stops, boldly voiced for a church would not do at all when transferred to a small room. In fact, the dulciana of the average church organ more nearly gives the effect desired from the chief foundation stop, rather than the open diapason. Everything is relative and we are dealing with fixed tones, which on an open sound-board cannot be modified, and in small rooms we may even prefer to obtain certain results synthetically.

The nominal "8ft." lengths vary greatly in reeds, and tubes of half length are much in evidence. The upper work will be made from one to three or four pipes smaller than the foundation stops on which it is built, pure string and flute tone being regarded as extraneous to the real tonal structure ; and, unless this principle is observed, an objectionable "sympathy" will be set up,—e.g., two open diapasons or two principals of the same scale and voicing will interfere with each other and sound no louder than one stop.

On the pedals, 12in. by 11in. is the usual scale for a pedal open, 9in. by 8in. for the bourdon, and 7in. by 5in. for a violone (all wood stops), at CCC. Zinc, 16ft. front, 10in. at CCC.

In an organ built by Messrs. Morten & Taylor, for the late Dr. Haynes, for Mistley Church, Essex, the following enormous scales were employed. *Great :* open diapason CC 9in., flûte à pavillon 8¼in. *Pedal :* open (wood) CCC across the mouth 16½in.; 19½in. by 21½in. (outside). *Pedal :* bourdon (wood) CCC across the mouth 11½in.; 14½in. by 16in. (outside).

The following measurements are taken from an old Robson organ ; one of the many reminders of the days when timber was good and there was no scarcity of it. *Pedal :* open CCC across the mouth 11¾in.; 14in. by 15½in. (outside). In cheap inferior work, one may find such stops so reduced in scale, substance and quality as to cost only about half what this scale would imply, carried through the entire range.

Very elaborate working diagrams for the making of any set of pipes to scale are given in Töpfer's book, but the reader will find these in a more condensed and practical form in Dr. Hinton's "Organ Construction."

' It is largely through the use of scales of generous proportions, combined with metal of good substance and quality that the organs of the best firms with the best reputation for fine tone are so much more expensive than those of less costly competitors. If organ committees could only look into the future a little when discussing tenders for new work, it would often pay them better to accept the highest rather than the lowest estimate. A personal experience will serve to illustrate the matter. Some years ago the author was asked to report on a new organ which disappointed the church authorities. The church was a large new one, and the architect had provided ample space for a suitable organ with two good arches facing south and west. On entering the organ chamber, the pipes appeared to have ample speaking room on sound-boards of fair size, and there was much spotted metal in evidence. Yet the great organ especially was quite lacking in dignity and impressiveness.

On closer examination it was evident that the metal, though good, was thin and the scales more suited to a chamber organ than one for a large church. As preparation was made for several stops on the choir, the obvious remedy was to advise the transference of certain "great" foundation stops to that department, entire substitution of others of heavier metal, and the shifting up of other stops, to increase the scale. All this, of course, involved an entire reconstruction of the building-up and balance of tone on the principal manual, at considerable extra cost. Merely to increase the wind pressure, regulating all over afresh, would not have availed here, for small scales and thin metal would not bear such treatment. In the choice of suitable scales lies most of the *individuality* which distinguishes the work of one high class firm from that of another. Taking, for example, three firms of the highest standing, but whose ideals in the matter of tone differ greatly,— Messrs. Willis, Walker, and Lewis; a player with a wide experience and a keen ear for tone would have little difficulty on entering a church in recognising a typical specimen of either, provided the instrument had not been much altered by another builder than the original one. The traditions are mostly maintained, though the voicers may change.*

People generally do not realise the great influence a building has upon the fixed tones of an organ. We may take a piano or a violin from a small room to a large one, and the sensitive fingers of the player can adapt themselves at once to the altered conditions. But an organ, scaled and delicately voiced as a chamber instrument becomes a mere toy in large and unsuitable surroundings. Re-voicing and loudening have their limitations, which, overstepped, only result in spoiling a stop too thin or too small in scale to bear more wind-pressure. Conversely, there have been instances of organs built for some large church, bought against expert advice, and placed in a much smaller one only to be removed within a short time on account of their unsuitability. In "Studies in Organ Tone" by the Rev. Noel A. Bonavia Hunt, the reader will find much of interest respecting the actual scales and treatment of the mouths of various stops. But here, perhaps, more than in any other matter connected with the organ, "a little knowledge is a dangerous thing," and amateurs in organ building should refrain from forcing upon any pipe maker any scales given in books without special reference to the position of the particular organ. For this he should seek expert advice.

---

* Since the above was written, some important amalgamations have taken place; Hill & Son with Norman & Beard, and Henry Willis & Sons with Lewis & Co. The effect on English organ building will be watched with interest.

The Manuals.

MODERN keyboards are made to over-hang and are placed closer as to height so that the player may use the device known as "thumbing" on the keyboard below. But many keyboards possess these serious faults, — the overhang is so great that in a rapid interchange of chords between the manuals, involving much employment of the black keys, the hands have to be drawn forward to clear the keyboard above, and the black keys are so close together that unless the player's fingers taper quite exceptionally he cannot play certain full chords without touching one or other of the "sharps." From the old - fashioned keyboards, with their absurdly wide spaces between C♯ and D♯, makers have gone to the other extreme, and would seem to have in mind chiefly lady organists. One meets with keys so faulty in this respect that the middle fingers are liable to become wedged between the F♯, G♯, and A♯ in full chords employ-ing every finger and requiring a forward position of the hand with the thumbs on C♯. In an article calling attention to these matters in 1913, Mr. E. H. Lemare declares the most comfortable and practicable keyboard he has ever played on to be in Cavaillé-Coll's organ in the Albert Hall, Shef-field, with the keys overhanging half-an-inch and the manuals brought closer together in height but not in depth, yet leaving space enough for the necessary thumb pistons. The well-known Guilmant Caprice in B♭ he considers was conceived for such a keyboard. At some recitals he has even changed pieces "rather than smudge certain passages or take a chance of injuring my knuckles on the usual sharp edges of the overhanging manual. Often it has been necessary to call in the assistance of the organ tuner, who, with sandpaper in hand, has smoothed off some of the danger overhead." This latter experience has also been mine; but, coming from a player so familiar with every type of organ as Mr. Lemare, it may be hoped that should any keymakers chance to read these lines they will reconsider their standards of measurement with a view to placing them beyond criticism.

There ought to be an absolutely fixed standard for key measurements, and players should demand it from builders and their keymakers. The normal measurement of an octave on the piano is $7\frac{3}{8}$ ins., and some organ builders, without the slightest regard for the organist's comfort and accuracy of technique, have actually so reduced the width in their "CC to C, seven octaves compass," that the sixty-one notes are got into the space of $\frac{5}{8}$ in. less than the proper distance,—nearly the width of one white key!

There also exists the horrible contrivance which seems expressly designed to fatigue the player, and ruin his sense of touch, which is known as "spring touch," which need only be mentioned here to be condemned and to warn players against permitting it to be placed in any future instrument.

In compass all new organs should extend to C, sixty-one notes. The upper notes are demanded in a great deal of modern music; and, if the player is limited to G or A, he must mutilate many passages when using one of the most beautiful effects

in a good modern organ,— a 16ft. stop with one or
more 8ft. played an octave higher. The value of
the octave coupler is also enhanced by the C compass.

Keymakers speak of the ivories as "12 cut,"
"16 cut," &c. By this they mean the number to
the inch ; the cost per set being from about £3 to
£5, according to quality and thickness. Although
ivory has been steadily increasing in cost for many
years past, it is well worth securing the thicker
gauge on the score of durability. Some of the best
substitutes are, however, quite excellent and possess this advantage,—that they do not turn yellow.
In the highest class work, as seen in many of
our cathedral and concert organs, the ivories are
cut out of one solid piece of exceptional thickness.

Keys are best kept clean with a few drops of
methylated spirit on a duster. An artist's touch is
a very sensitive thing, and there is always a sense
of discomfort, which must react on his playing
when confronted with manuals encrusted with dirt
or sticky through damp. The late Mr. W. T. Best
would never think of giving a recital on any organ
without first carefully wiping the keys.

For the front edges there exist many patterns,
but this is chiefly a matter of appearance. Thick
sharps, sloping backward a good deal, and with
circular fronts, at one time so much in evidence, chiefly in English pianos, need only be mentioned to be condemned.

With the ever increasing facilities offered for
stop control, the fifth manual of certain large
organs may be regarded as a doubtful blessing,
and will probably be one day condemned on
account of the eye-strain caused through placing
the desk too high and too far away. With a view
to the player's comfort, enabling him to keep his
forearm in correct line with each manual, some
modern organs of three or four manuals have the

swell and solo tilted upward and choir downward. Though the appearance is odd, the increase in comfort is undeniable.

The excellent and practical notes given in "Repairing the Pianoforte" on the "Mode of Manufacture," "Recovering with Celluloid," "Scraping and Polishing Ivories," and "Repinning Keys," will give the reader all the further information he needs concerning this section of our subject.

The Pedal Board.

THE old flat pedal board has practically disappeared, and organists are unanimous in favour of concavity, but not with regard to radiation, so that it will be best here to give both sides of the case, merely noting in passing that radiation without concavity, occasionally met with, is an abomination that no builder of to-day, one hopes, would dream of perpetuating.

Mr. W. T. Best, whose pedal technique — acquired mostly on the old flat pedal board of his early days — has never been excelled, in 1881 declared himself as follows :—

"As to the principle of 'radiation,' experience has taught me to hold it in light estimation. Passages which frequently occur, requiring a 'crossing of the feet' on the long keys, are rendered almost impossible and always hazardous by the diminishing gauge. Unless the pedals radiate very slightly, which is hardly ever the case, I prefer the usual plan,—and may here add that I am in favour of the middle D of the pedals being under middle C of the keyboard, particularly when the former extends to F or G. This arrangement divides the pedal range better."

The radiation, taken from a radius of 8ft., as found in ½most of our cathedral organs, appears to many as excessive and is being modified. On the other side, it may be claimed that the toe and heel playing at the extreme ends is facilitated by radiation. Mr. J. J. Binns, who supplies only radiating and concave pedal boards (the radiation being taken from a modified radius of 12ft. 6in.), states his other measurements as follows, in agreement with the revised R.C.O. measurements :—

" 1. Position of pedal board central with keys CC to C and remaining in that position if only up to G or A.

" 2. Height for two or three manuals, 31 in. from top of centre pedal to top of lowest row of keys when up to touch.

" 3. Radius of concavity, 8ft. 6in.; radius of sharps, 8ft. 1in.; radius of radiation, 12ft. 6in.

4. Sharps all equal lengths, 5in. on top side from radial toe rail."

Oak, teak and birch are the hard woods suitable for pedal boards, the latter being used in the great majority of organs.

In Germany, the old pedal boards extended usually only to D, 27 notes; sometimes to E; were of course flat, and to suit the heavier build of the Germans were of much wider gauge than those of any English maker. Such pedal boards naturally favour alternate foot playing rather than the use of the toe and heel, which is sometimes called by the Germans "artistic pedal playing." Merkel once stated that the finest pedal player he had ever known was, strangely enough, a Russian (for there are very few organs in Russia), who used alternate feet exclusively, but added that it was carrying matters to an extreme.

Mr. Vincent Willis, in his most interesting experimental organ at Brentford, introduced a novel form of pedal board so levered that instead of the ordinary pin at the back and spring in front the depth of touch remained the same throughout the length of each pedal key. It feels quite agreeable to the player, but until actually introduced into some important instrument has but little chance of making its way. In a letter to me (April, 1917), Mr. Willis comments thus on the conservatism of players :—

"The great popularity of organ recitals led me to think that organists would welcome any means which facilitated the manipulation of the organ. I very soon had cause to remember that my father had to apply his 1851 thumb pistons, as it were, on sufferance for thirty years before their value was firmly established, and that the Wesley-Willis pedal board was rejected by the R.C.O. to find a belated reconsideration and acceptance by that institution a year later."

It is characteristic of "Verbotenland" that all console measurements are, or were, absolutely fixed by law, which Herr Otto Dienel considered a hindrance to progress. Certainly it would have so acted with us if the R.C.O. regulations of 1881 (since withdrawn) had been similarly enforced.

Experiments have been made for placing short keys ("sharps") also at the back for occasional use by the heel in certain troublesome passages. This innovation would be more likely to come into use if Mr. V. Willis's idea of an uniform depth of touch were given the extended trials it deserves. His patent says :—

"The pedal key, in any type of pedal board, is a lever hinged or fulcrummed under the organist, free to move a convenient distance or 'touch' at the front of the 'sharp' key. Midway between the front of the sharp and the hinge, therefore, the travel is halved, and the effort required from the foot at that point doubled. As the feet must often be crossed in pedal playing, a considerable length of key is used, and although much practice has made the player unconscious of the unequal effort or travel, it is an adverse condition that should be removed. And as the average touch must be adequate, that of the sharp keys is unnecessarily deep, requiring a height of sharp that throws a needless strain on the flexibility of the foot. To overcome these imperfections, I secure a parallel or equal travel for the pedal by means of coupled levers, bell cranks or other suitable means. The whole of the natural key now becomes equally useful, and the necessity for crossing the feet near the sharp vanishes. The equal sharp permits a lower sharp key and a more natural position and action of the foot. Given a parallel travel to the pedal key, many possibilities appear. The sharp keys may be duplicated and played with the heel. The pedal key-board, with duplicated sharps, may be divided centrally and transversely and two separate pedal boards become a reality. Two short pedal-boards may be arranged one behind the other, with the sharps in the usual position."

These suggestions open out a wide field for experiment and foreshadow the possibility of a new pedal technique for a future race of players.

Systems of Control.

THE usual mechanical arrangement of double acting pedals with iron trundles set in a hardwood frame does not seem likely to be superseded for small tracker organs. Two manuals up to six stops on each require two pedals to each; up to ten stops three each, and for twelve stop sound-boards builders should specify four.

Thumb pistons can be successfully applied to almost any tracker organ, on a wind pressure of only 3in.; but it must be seen that there is no stiffness in the slides or the pistons will be of little use to the player. The old mechanical arrangement looks clumsy and cumbersome beside a well-finished and compact pneumatic draw-stop action. Organs of from thirty to forty speaking stops should have five or six of these pistons for great and swell and four for the choir. Three or four of them ought to give suitable gradations of tone, whilst the others would be best placed a little apart from these, giving special "solo" combinations not instantaneously obtainable at the stop jambs. For example. *Great :* trumpet only and 4ft. flute only. *Swell :* voix célestes and gamba, oboe or horn solo.

An important pedal organ is best controlled by pedal compositions, as in some of Mr. Henry Willis's large concert organs, which should, however, be pneumatic like the rest of the action of any large organ.

Messrs. Lewis & Co. prefer to insert a system of key touches, — little ivory projections above the key-board affected. But, while bearing testimony to the fine work of this firm, the system of thumb pistons as originally introduced by Mr. Henry Willis seems more natural, and appears to be preferred by players to any upward and forward movement of the fingers.

The Hope-Jones organs also have the forward arrangement for the stop keys, yet the inventor admitted in conversation that the action of the thumb under the manual in use was best; but that, having adopted the "forward" touch of the finger, they continued to do so for the sake of uniformity.

Mr. J. J. Binns has a very clever patent pneumatic device for immediate adjustment at the console. He usually provides three interchangeable combination pedals for each manual. In the draw-stop jambs above each group of stops are three stop-knobs. Any stop or group of stops belonging to the great, for example, when drawn becomes fixed on No. 1 pedal by simply pulling out No. 1 stop knob and letting it return by its spring. Then, pushing in these stops, any others (or part of the same group if desired) become fixed on No. 2 pedal by merely pulling them out and registering them in the same way, and so on with No. 3. Every time a special combination knob is drawn it attaches to its corresponding pedal the stops that are out at the time. The mechanism is, of course, pneumatic; and if one has a good memory such a system helps a recitalist greatly, enabling him to render with ease pieces requiring unusual combinations. It is a fair question and one depending largely upon personal idiosyncracies whether three of these pedals instantaneously adjustable are preferable to, let us say, five "fixed" pistons, or pistons which can be adjusted (though not with the same facility) during performance.

Another method of fixing combinations on the pedals which has sometimes been employed both in England and France utilises the draw-stop rod itself, which on being drawn is given a half turn to the right, thereby fixing the stop to a pedal. As the idea is obviously practical by purely mechanical means, it would be worth while if some skilful mechanic would develop it further and render it available for small organs with few composition pedals.

The modern German *Rollschweller*, a wheel in the centre of the front board turned by the foot, makes a *crescendo* of the entire organ without acting on the stop knobs themselves. It has not been used to any great extent in English organs; but in the fine instrument by Messrs. J. W. Walker & Sons, in York Minster (1903), a grand *crescendo* pedal was introduced. The control is as follows:—

"Electro-pneumatic pistons, eight great, six swell, four solo, three choir, eight pedal, and six for duplicating the swell pistons on the pedal. All these are adjustable.

"(A) Double-acting pedal controlling great to pedal coupler.

"(B) Coupler great pistons to pedal combinations.

"(C) Pedal basses to swell organ, whereby the pedal organ may be controlled in suitable combinations (not necessarily the same as those associated with the great) by either the swell pistons or combination pedals.

"By drawing B, leaving C undrawn, the great and pedal stops are simultaneously controlled by either pistons or pedals. By leaving B undrawn the pistons affect the great organ stops only, and combination pedals affect the pedal stops only. The swell combination pedals being simply duplicates of the swell pistons do not affect the pedal organ unless C is drawn, which controls six grades of pedal tone, appropriate to the swell combinations.

"There is also a grand *crescendo* pedal bringing on the piston and pedal combinations from soft to full, affecting also the solo tubas, great to pedal, swell to great, and solo to great couplers, in appropriate order, thus enabling the player to increase his organ from soft to full, or *vice versâ*, or to arrest the *crescendo* at any point without touching a stop or piston, and so arranged as to leave all pistons, &c., free to work as usual directly the foot is removed."

The piston fans and stop connections are in full view and are easily accessible on opening a panel beside the console. Any alteration can be effected by the turn of a button on a plainly marked rod.

In the concert organ at the Royal College of Music, South Kensington, built in 1901, Messrs. Walker introduced an ingenious system of pointers or switches, acting as follows in connection with sixteen electro-pneumatic pistons and pedals and two selective pistons:— *210972*

"The pointers to the left of swell stops and to the right of the great stops are switches which connect the stops of these manuals to their respective selective piston.

"In a horizontal line with each stop is an ivory dot. If the pointer is directed to the dot the stop is pushed out, and if the pointer is directed away from the dot upwards the stop is pushed in, when the selective piston is used.

"The pointers to the left of the pedal stops are switches, which connect the pedal stops to the great organ selective piston only.

"*Note.*—The four ordinary pistons of great and

swell organs and the pedal composition pedals are entirely independent of the selective pistons and are in no way affected by them.

"The selective pistons are intended to supply the player with the means of arranging a special combination or a solo effect on either great or swell organs, and may therefore be considered simply as an added facility, not necessarily brought into use for ordinary playing."

Some remarkable possibilities of control are indicated in a patent of Mr. Vincent Willis's dated so far back as 1898, — possibilities which ought long ago to have been fully developed and tested in some important instrument. Its nature can only be briefly alluded to here. Its chief feature consists in making the draw-stop respond to a touch of the finger upon the knob and, whether in or out, automatically effecting the operation required. The draw-stop is made

"its own reversing key, with the object of causing the draw-stop when touched to follow the finger to the extent of its travel if in, or to retreat from the finger if out; a momentary touch, therefore, is all that is required from the organist to reverse the position of the draw stop, and he is relieved of the anxiety of selecting the right spot. The organist can arrange any succeeding combination by simply touching the draw-stops, which will not re-arrange themselves until the controlling device is operated and the energy required to move the drawstop is free to do so. The actual condition of the organ is always indicated by the position of the draw-stops."

This, if capable of realisation at not too prohibitive an expense, would appear to be the last word in pneumatic control.

In electro-pneumatics, Mr. Henry Willis, junr., has patented (1916) a *crescendo* device which operates through pressing down a projecting pedal. Stops are then automatically added to those already out, and the rate of speed is determined by a cam arrangement. The release of the pedal checks the addition of stops. Provision is, of course, made for reversing the process by a *decrescendo* pedal. This patent will be applied to the organ the firm is building for Liverpool Cathedral, and it should prove an effectual solution of the problem of building up a well graduated *crescendo* on organs of the largest type, whilst both hands and feet are taxed to their utmost. All stops and couplers can be controlled. If, as would appear from a study of the patent, the player is able to set the mechanism at varying speeds, its value would be much enhanced. The wheel device found in large modern American and German organs must be kept moving with the foot, and does not throw out the stops, whereas these new *crescendo* and *decrescendo* pedals hitch down and act on the stops. The release of either pedal arrests its automatic action, so that in the control of a very large organ the player will be practically relieved of all anxiety.

Couplers.

THE indispensable couplers are those uniting the manuals to the pedals, the swell to the great, and the great to the choir. "Choir to great" is sometimes useful in very incomplete and sketchy three-manual organs, and a choir suboctave to great may be regarded as a sort of apology for the absence of a double on that key-board. A swell octave on itself is more useful than a great to swell octave sometimes met with. Sub-octave couplers are perhaps best avoided in tracker work, for the extra mechanism adds to the weight of touch, and eventually leads to noise and liability to cipher. In pneumatic work these objections do not hold good; but an organ with many couplers and few speaking stops is at best a disappointing affair, its console arousing expectations which are not fulfilled.

The modern "unison off" (if the organ is pneumatic or electro-pneumatic) is a most useful modern addition to the swell octave and suboctave couplers; for unison pitch being silenced, these couplers, singly or together, are capable of producing new effects, especially from the reeds.

Messrs. Harrison & Harrison, of Durham, make a novel use of the "unison off" coupler. At Ely, Wells, and St. Mary's, Glasgow, the clarinet is of 16ft. pitch. A piston gives the player this stop at 8ft. pitch by acting simultaneously on the octave coupler and the "unison off."

The swell to great coupler may be made to unite the manuals in various ways mechanically, usually either by short backfalls or by wedging the keys at the tail end, as in the "ram's head" type. There are probably few survivals of an objectionable form known as the "tumbler" coupler, which entailed lifting the hands from the great as one drew it. Old German organs frequently united the upper manual to the one below it by drawing the upper manual about half-an-inch towards the player, a couple of brass knobs being provided for that purpose at each end of the key frame. It could also be pushed to and fro whilst playing. French builders frequently assign coupling movements to hitch-down pedals, where the English organist would expect to find composition pedals. All the "tracker" forms of coupling, of course, add the weight of touch of the keyboard coupled; and here the pneumatic action shows to great advantage, as in the best modern types the touch remains unaltered.

For coupling manuals to pedals, the roller-board is generally used for every type of organ, as being still the most simple and direct, unless balanced swell pedals occupy the centre of the front board.

The late Mr. T. Casson was a strong advocate for placing the manual couplers underneath the department they augmented,—e.g., the swell to great beneath the great organ stops, and so on; but only a few builders have adopted this system, which, on the whole, does not possess any real advantage over the usual plan of grouping them on the left-hand side.

The *sforzando* pedal is a useful addition to the resources of large four-manual organs, a touch of the pedal temporarily uniting any stops that may be drawn on the solo manual to the great for the purpose of accent.

Tubular Pneumatics.

IN these actions diminutive bellows of the diagonal type, inflated through small lead tubing, opening and closing discs or valves of cardboard and felt, take the place of trackers, squares and backfalls. A great advantage is gained, with a corresponding drawback. The touch of the largest organ may indeed be as light as we please—often it has been made far too light so that the slightest accidental touch or the mere falling of a single sheet of music on the keys will cause them to speak—but, however pleasant and silent, it never seems quite so *intimate* to the player as a really well laid out and carefully bushed tracker action.

Other advantages that may reasonably be claimed for a good tubular pneumatic action are these: the key levels do not alter, there are not so many centres of friction to cause noise as time goes on, and (always provided the situation is not too damp for the motors) the organist will seldom need to do anything in the way of regulating its moving parts.

Should a cipher occur, there is a little button on the top of the motor for regulating, or the wire passing up through the pneumatic box may have corroded and need lubricating with a touch of vaseline. Another cause may exist within the sound-board, and (as is sometimes the case with ordinary tracker work) the spring may not be quite strong enough to return the pallet. The remedy is to take it out with the pallet spring tool made for the purpose and, holding it by the bowl, pulling the ends a little further apart with a pair of pliers.

The air already in the tubes is merely pushed on by the key impulse; but, since the air is elastic, about thirty feet is regarded as the limit in length or the response will be slow.

The accompanying sketch shows the application of tubular pneumatics to the front pipes :—

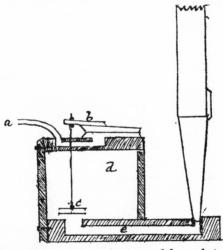

(a) is the tube from the sound-board, transmitting a puff of air into the little outside motor (b), thereby raising the circular disc or valve (c). The pneumatic chest (d) is supplied with wind direct from the main bellows or reservoir by a two inch wind trunk (not shown) placed at one side or in any convenient position. The disc (c) being lifted wind from (d) passes along the channel (e) to the foot of the pipe. The great sound-board is thus relieved of the heavy demand for wind made by the 8ft. and 16ft. metal basses. Sometimes, the motor (*b*) is placed underneath the pneumatic box, pushing up the inside valve instead of drawing it up, but the main principle is here the same.

But the reader will find in many cases that the motors are placed inside the pneumatic box, and that builders have exercised much ingenuity with regard to their arrangement. Instead of being inflated, they may be made to collapse or exhaust by the compressed air on their external surfaces pressing them down. We have then action by deflation, preferred in many cases. The next figure shows pneumatic action applied to the pedals. Here by a simple lever (*a*) the downward movement of the pedal is converted into one pushing up the valve (*b*), which is returned by a spring inside the pneumatic box. The tube (*c*) leads to the pedal sound-board, which is of course pneumatic. If any of the front pipes are 16ft. or 8ft. pedal basses, these tubes would be carried to the pneumatic chest, as shown behind the front in the previous sketch.

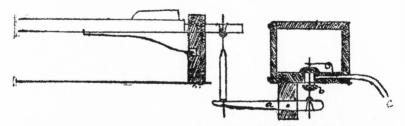

These tubes should be bound together for their mutual protection with wide tape wherever it is possible to do so. One sometimes finds them spread about carelessly and a dumb note may be traced to a tube that has been bent or trodden on so that the air impulse is checked in its passage. It will then have to be cut, rounded out and joined together again or a small piece of larger tubing passed over the ends. To fasten a bunch of tubes to any wooden support, a few inches of spare tubing flattened out is generally used.

These illustrations show pneumatics in their simplest forms, easily understood by the reader. As thus used for fronts and pedals, they are freely applied to "tracker" organs as well as to those which are entirely pneumatic. To explain fully the different actions of our leading builders a whole book on the subject would be needed.

Readers specially interested in the subject will find other systems illustrated in Dr. Hinton's "Catechism of the Organ" (Weekes & Co.), showing Wedlake's "Eclipse" pneumatic with flexible seated valve; Bryceson's patent; the principles of deflation and inflation compared; and Schmole & Mol's electro-pneumatic. And in a "Handbook of the Organ" (Augener Ltd.) illustrations of Binns's patent and the Hope-Jones electro-pneumatic system. The "floating lever," a patent of Mr. V. Willis's (1884), though no longer used by the firm, deserves passing mention by reason of its ingenuity. The name was given it at the Inventions Exhibition of 1885, where it was awarded a gold medal. A lever in the middle of the mechanism, instead of being centred, was suspended or poised, the buttons at either end, connected with backfall and valve, serving as temporary fulcrums. About half-a-dozen Willis organs, including Truro Cathedral, were supplied with it; but, although exceedingly prompt in action, it was found costly in manufacture and difficult to regulate, so that the firm prefers using another form of the Barker-Willis lever. An illustration of the "floating lever" may be found in the "National Encyclopædia," vol. x., plate 3.

The Tremulant.

NO organ effect is so much abused as this, and in small country church organs played chiefly by amateurs it is best omitted from a specification. In small buildings which are devoid of resonance, it is particularly objectionable and a player who can endure one with a very strong beat from beginning to end of a piece reminds one all too painfully of our friend Mr. La T. Soll of the music halls, who never opens his lips without bleating like a goat! However, under favourable conditions, a tremulant with a quiet refined beat is a perfectly legitimate addition to the resources of an organ if used with artistic restraint.

The old form shown in most books, with a projecting rod weighted on the top, is a very inferior kind, noisy, uncertain in action and wasteful of wind.

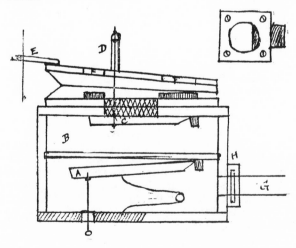

An organ possessing a tremulant should also have a separate reservoir for the swell, else the great and pedal are also subject to the beat. If it can be placed inside the swell box, to lessen its noise in working, it is a decided advantage, or when convenient it may be fastened against a solid wall. The tube from reservoir to wind chest should be two inches in diameter. As tremulants require regulating from time to time, and are apt occasionally to "race" and "thump," it is desirable to fit a slide of hard wood to the side of the box, on the principle of a magic lantern slide, so that the amount of wind admitted into the box may be controlled. Attempts have been made to control the speed of the beat, so that it increases and diminishes with the opening and closing of the swell shutters, but they have not been brought into general use. This could be effected by a pedal pulling out the slide shown in the drawing, limiting the amount of travel to about $\frac{3}{4}$in. Messrs. Henry Willis & Sons have something of the kind in their latest examples. The tremulant should not be operated by a draw stop, but by a hitch-down pedal to the right; and if angles are awkward for a mechanical action by tracker and square, it can easily be fitted with a pneumatic starting arrangement.

One of the best forms is that shown in the accompanying sketch. The size of the box is 20in. and 8in. by 8in. and the thickness should not be less than $\frac{7}{8}$in. There are two compartments, the tube from the sound-board entering the lower division. The pallet A being opened by its pull-down, wind rushes into the upper division, B. The pallet C in the upper division has a tapped wire running through it to the bridge, D; double buttons being provided for regulation. There are two vents in the feeder on the top of the box, exhausting the wind automatically. Thus filling and emptying in regular pulsations, the wind inside the wind chest is also agitated rhythmically on its way to the pipes above.

It is sometimes necessary to screw a lead weight across the top of the feeder to slow down the beat. If the tremulant rests on or is screwed against some thick strips of felt, it will be the less likely to communicate its vibration to any adjacent mechanism, and it should never be placed near the player. It will sometimes set the long rollers of an iron roller-board rattling. A few stouter pins through the studs at the end of each roller may remedy this; but if they are too close, a slip or two of the thinnest kid may be interlaced between the rollers where they touch each other. As a means of expression, it can never approach the perfectly controllable vibrato of the violinist, but modern improvements may be said to justify its existence.

At the end of the feeder is shown a simple regulating device, E,—a piece of wood tipped with felt screwed into any adjacent support. It is sometimes effective in lessening the "thump," but the beat is best regulated by means of a slide as shown at H (and also separately shown at top of illustration), on the principle of a magic lantern slide; for the size of the tube, G, entering the box, is purely a matter of empirical guesswork, affected by several varying factors. Great changes in the atmospheric conditions often make a little regulation desirable, and by this means it can be done in a moment. Sometimes a fine spiral spring of steel with tapped wire and button through a slip of wood projecting from the end of the feeder and hooked to the top of the box has been used to regulate and quieten the beat.

The Swell Box.

THE swell box should not be less than two inches in thickness, and it should be lined with stout brown paper. They are sometimes framed up with thinner matched boards and packed with sawdust; but the former plan is, in the author's opinion, preferable, especially if one inch boards are screwed together, with a thick layer of felt-paper between. As the effectiveness of a swell box is due not only to the successful diminution of the tone when the box is closed but also to its successful expulsion when the shutters are open, it is probable that a hard, polished, enamelled surface would help considerably; for sound is reflected in much the same way as the rays of light are, and it has been proved (as anyone might have foreseen) that soft, absorbent felt material of any kind as a lining to the inside is most injurious to the tone.

THE SHUTTERS.

If we leave a door slightly ajar, anyone outside can hear what is going on within the room almost as well as if the door were wide open. So it is with swell shutters: they *must* fit closely to obtain the distant effect. When, through careless fitting or the shrinking of unseasoned wood this is not the case, a very material improvement can be effected by lining the inside of each shutter with stout brown paper, overlapping the top edge of

each shutter, which may need two or three thicknesses or a renewal of the white leather or felt on
the under edge with thicker material. Probably
a little glue with the paste will be needed to make
the brown paper adhere well, if it is too absorbent.

Primitive forms of the swell box consisted
either in a box with the top made to open or
perpendicular sliding panels. This latter form is
even now sometimes used with very fair results in
small chamber organs designed for ordinary drawing rooms, wherein every inch of space that can
be saved is a consideration.

The horizontal or vertical shutters of modern
organs are usually about ten inches wide. The
horizontal shutter closes naturally, almost with its
own weight, and it is rarely necessary to take out
the whole eight or ten for tuning purposes (as in
the case of vertical shutters, which must be closed
pneumatically or by springs, with a less feeling of
security against any after movement of the
shutters).

Organ music, especially arrangements, abounds
in *crescendo* and *decrescendo* marks, which cannot
be properly played by either style of swell pedal
without seriously interfering with the pedal passage underneath, however adroit the player's left
foot may be ; so that he must frequently choose
between disregarding these dynamic signs entirely
or crippling the pedal passage. Many years
ago, the late Mr. Henry Willis placed a pneumatic
tube with a mouthpiece for the player's use to control the swell shutters in one of his organs, so that
the following suggestion should be quite feasible,—
viz., that builders should provide two thumb pistons
to open and close the swell shutters gradually
and automatically, or a single reversible piston.
One thumb could often be spared for an instant
whilst both feet are engaged in rapid pedalling.
At any rate, the present crude arrangement found

in most English organs of a pedal which causes the player's feet to lose some valuable seconds in a quick movement, because of the need of guiding the pedal all the way on its return lest the shutters close with a bang should no longer be tolerated by players and by those who design organs.

Sometimes one finds the pins uniting the shutters to the upright rod work out through not being secured at the end by thread and button. When that is the case, it is a simple matter to obtain from an ironmonger screws of a suitable gauge with the heads turned at right angles; and a few buttons may easily be cut out of scraps of leather one-eighth inch thick, and thus render it impossible for the swell to be put out of action. The pins, and possibly the ends of the shutters and other moving parts, will need an occasional lubrication with tallow to prevent squeaking.

The horizontal variety made to open the reverse way, throwing the tone upwards to the roof, is only suitable under exceptional conditions and cannot be considered a model for general adoption, for much dust will thereby be thrown into the reeds that would otherwise be excluded. Just as a lean-to roof in an organ chamber reflects the tone across the chancel, so does a sloping top to the swell box assist the expulsion of sound. Too large a box is as much a fault as one that is too small. If we placed a few stops on a sound-board in some large adjacent room, fitting swell shutters to the opening, we could obtain a very distant effect, yet a poor *crescendo* through lack of compression. On the other hand, a large number of stops crowded into a box which is too small, if played on for any length of time with the shutters closed, will actually be put out of tune for the time by the heated and compressed air finding no vent.

The old builders frequently left the bass octave

of their 16ft. bourdons outside the box: they should always be included. Mitreing does little harm and is often unavoidable. The gamba or viol open basses are frequently turned over with a perpendicular mitre, but they are voiced accordingly. A passage way down the centre or free access at the back is necessary when there are nine or more stops to tune. The reeds are usually placed for convenience next to the shutters, and three reed stops are as many as a tuner can be expected to reach without standing room between them and the flue work.

In large organs, very effective boxes are built up of brick or concrete, and the latter material being hard and unyielding would make an excellent box set in a hard wood frame and made up in slabs properly overlapping or dovetailed, for $1\frac{1}{2}$in. thickness would be ample. In view of the greatly increased cost and scarcity of timber, experiments in this direction would be well worth while. Often a hole in the back of the box will make little or no difference to its effectiveness, the main thing being the accurate fit of the shutters. Shutters controlled by electro-pneumatic action are sometimes made to open rapidly one after the other, and such swell boxes may be at a great distance from the player. A notable example is the very delicate fourteen stop echo organ (playable from a fifth manual) at Norwich Cathedral, where it is placed in the apse at the extreme east end.

Attempts have been made in America in the direction of enclosing practically every department of the organ in swell boxes; and Mr. G. A. Audsley in his book on the organ says: "We unhesitatingly affirm, on all grounds of art and taste, that the great organ as an *absolute* and *unexpressive* division should neither be looked upon as the most important and useful nor be made the loudest and most assertive part of the instrument." It is safe to say that no European player or builder of note would endorse this dogmatic utterance, for it is a well-known fact that, even under very favourable conditions, a swell box robs open diapasons—the most valuable class of stops in every organ—of a good deal of their quality of tone. The most glorious sounds that can proceed from an organ come, after all, from these in some great and lofty cathedral, and were they all enclosed or made to assume some quite secondary feature in the *ensemble* our finest organs would be sadly marred.

Reed and string are the two classes of stops which are most effective behind swell shutters, for they are the richest in upper partials, and these overtones are greatly influenced by the *crescendo* and *diminuendo*. The large scale weighty foundation tone we require from the great is costly and wasteful inside the swell box; from this department we require brilliance, and there is a good deal to be said in favour of the violin diapason type as the chief open flue stop, together with the modern practice of extending the oboe to 16ft. CCC for the first double, instead of the usual lieblich bourdon. Better still, of course, if an independent contra fagotta 16ft. of small scale can be afforded; however softly voiced, it will be certain to tell and add greatly to the richness of the full swell.

Lever *v.* Balanced Swell Pedals.

T HIS controversy is by no means at an end, —each system has its partisans. The lever form is more certain in its working, being rather easier to close accurately, without being liable to be jerked open again on the release of the foot, as the horizontal shutters close with their own weight. It would be still more efficient if builders would, as a matter of course, arrange for it to return automatically at a suitable speed when the player has pressed it down to the farthest limit so as to allow him to withdraw the foot hastily without having to guide it up all the way to avoid the banging of the shutters. Mr. Henry Willis gave the organist this advantage many years ago at the Alexandra Palace, and it adds much life to the playing.

The rod holding down the pedal may be made either to swing free of it or to pass through the iron itself, and the player should not be expected to exert almost his whole power to press the pedal down as in some badly set out actions.

The balanced swell pedal is usually associated with vertical shutters, although the horizontal shutter can be, and often is, retained in rebuilds when the right foot lever pedal is discarded. The balanced pedal is placed in the centre of the front board, to the unavoidable derangement of the coupling mechanism, "stabbing the organ in a vital place," to quote one opponent. The manual to pedal actions are sometimes arranged pneumatic-ally, without taking down the keys, when, of course, this objection does not apply. But most players like "to see the keys go down" when coupling to pedals, and the mechanical roller-board and pull-down action is usually preferred. Although a notched rod has been contrived with the lever form allowing the player some choice as to grad-ations of tone, the balanced form has undoubtedly the advantage here, for a very slight touch with the toe or heel of either foot will give him just the amount of fixed tone he temporarily desires. And when there are two departments in swell boxes—swell and choir or swell and solo—it is very con-venient to be able to operate them simultaneously with the same foot. Pedalling with the left foot only is discouraged. Certain passages seem more comfortably performed with the balanced swell, others with the lever form; and, apparently in recognition of this fact, Dr. Alcock in his excellent organ method gives special exercises for each. The concert hall organ at the Royal College of Music, Kensington, built by Messrs. Walker & Sons, contains both forms of pedal. To bring the lever pedal into use it is necessary to close the front by the balanced pedal and draw a stop labelled "Swell lever pedal."

Endeavouring to set out controversial matters as fairly as possible, the author has no violent pre-judice one way or the other, only observing that when the balanced form is badly constructed it becomes a greater nuisance than any lever pedal is ever likely to be.

Tuning.

ACCURATE tuning is only possible after the touch has been so regulated that the pallets all open to their full extent, giving the pipes their full flush of wind. It is also assumed that each stop has been made even as to power throughout its entire compass. (See Regulation.) If we could keep our organs in a temperature of from 55 deg. to 60 deg. their well-being would be greatly enhanced, but that is in most cases an unattainable ideal. The climate of the British Isles is so variable that organs are often subject to anything between 40 deg. and 70 deg. When possible it is advisable to select a day in the summer months when the thermometer stands at 60 deg. and in the winter months at 55 deg. The reader will, it is assumed, know what is meant by "equal temperament" and the necessity of laying the "bearings" upon the principal. To avoid injury to the pipes a learner should first experiment either with an octave of pipes having slides or with one having stoppers. Only after considerable experience has been gained should an attempt be made to lay the bearings on a good organ (thereby disturbing every stop in relation to the principal), for instruments have suffered much more from inexperienced hands and too cheap tuning contracts than from hard practising thereon.

A portable electric light should be secured wherever practicable, and it is well to remind the reader at the start that metal pipes are extremely sensitive, — a light too near, much handling, or even the heat of the body will quickly sharpen the pitch, upsetting his subsequent pitch, unless he allows them about twenty minutes or so to cool. Having learnt to appreciate the sound of a fifth dead in tune, he will learn that the whole secret of laying bearings lies in the knowing just how much to flatten that interval without disturbing its relation to the octaves subsequently tested with it, and without altering the original or normal pitch of the entire organ.

The great principal being drawn, we must satisfy ourselves that the pipe C, third space treble clef, represents the true pitch of the entire organ, and we must be careful not to disturb this, our pitch note.

There are two or three different schemes, but the following one—testing with the octave—may be considered the safest and most accurate for general use. All schemes aim at this result: to make the octaves perfect, major thirds a little sharper than perfect, minor third a little flatter, fifths also flatter, and fourths in similar degree sharper than perfect. Accuracy in estimating these minute differences will come with patience and perseverance, given a good ear.

The white notes show those tuned, the black notes those to be tempered,—the fifth, G, being first brought dead into tune, and then so slightly flattened that slow waves are noticeable. The fifths are numbered in the above scheme 1 to 8. Continuing the scheme, we should get G♯ to D♯; D♯ to A♯; A♯ [B♭] to F; and F to C to complete the octave. But it is then preferable to return and take them in reverse order, C (third space) to F below, first making the F perfect and then sharpening it to the same degree as the upward fifth was previously flattened :—

Frequent testing with chords in all the keys will be necessary before a perfect result is obtained ; and the novice will have to be careful not to heat the pipes (thereby sharpening) by remaining too close to them for any length of time, or he will find it needful to go over a good deal of work again. Only old hands realise how sensitive small metal pipes are in this respect. The ear also soon tires and requires a rest, when a few chords on a quiet stop of the dulciana type will afford a grateful relief and ensure greater accuracy than if the tuner attempts to keep going for hours at a stretch.

The swell and choir may either have their bearings laid separately, after careful proving with middle C of the great principal on their own 4ft. stop; or, if the tuner is in a position to hear the pipes on both sound-boards equally well, the entire organ may be tuned from the great principal. But whatever plan is adopted, it will be found that

large scale flute stops will give a certain amount
of trouble, as they are often drawn into apparent
consonance by the principal; yet when tested with
a diapason or other 8ft. stop are not in agreement,
although we have carefully tuned the latter to the
principal. The statement "things which are equal
to the same thing are equal to one another" does
not apply to organ tuning!

The remedy lies in "cross-tuning" a clarabella
or harmonic flute on one of the diapasons, and a
4ft. flute may again be profitably run through with
the fifteenth. There is a certain latitude with
regard to the dissonant beats,—between their dis-
appearance on the flat side and their reappearance
on the sharp; and it is in accurately gauging this
centre that smooth and pure tuning lies, for we
must aim at a result which will stand reasonable
changes of temperature. When that change reaches
10 degrees, the player becomes unpleasantly re-
minded that his organ is no longer agreeable to
play on; and the reeds, at any rate, will certainly
need going through, because the rest of the metal
work will have either sharpened with heat or
flattened with cold.

Tuning cones should be touched over with a
little vaseline previous to use, and a small camel-
hair brush is useful in brushing out the mouths of
little pipes that have become choked through
dust. There is a special mixture cone tapering
more narrowly than the others. It is best to begin
at the bottom of the scale, with all very small
ranks of pipes, in order to educate the ear to
appreciate the pitch of the shrill trebles. By
shading the pipe with the point of the cone we
learn, when the ear is momentarily in doubt,
whether it requires flattening or sharpening. If
any pipes are bent over, they must be taken out
and gently rolled. Often that is the cause of a
small pipe being dumb,—the mouth bent inward

by some previous heavy treatment. Mixtures are best tuned after all the other flue work and the reeds last, as we have usually to lean over these to reach the other stops. The mixture ranks are separated by drawing out a pin at the end of the slider, and this is preferable to the use of small mops to silence the ranks we do not desire to have sounding. On replacing the pin, the work done should be tested by drawing all the open foundation work in full chords in various keys, when perhaps a note or two may stand out and require re-touching.

The voix célestes consist of two ranks of string-toned pipes, one rank being slightly sharpened. It may be of the mild dulciana or vox angelica type, or the salicional (with a little more character), or the more pungent gamba, or the still keener viol d'orchestre,—a certain amount of stringiness is essential. The author has a strong predilection for the salicional type.

The late Herman Smith devoted much research and philosophical speculation to the subject of tuning, the result of which may be found in his "Modern Organ Tuning." The chapters in Elliston's "Organs and Tuning" and Dr. Hinton's "Organ Construction" are amongst the most valuable in those respective works and may be profitably perused by those who desire to study the subject thoroughly.

Borrowing or Transmission.

WE will deal first with borrowing that is perfectly legitimate; where it is indeed both foolish and wasteful not to avail ourselves of a plan which, whilst increasing our resources, saves both space and money. That department is the pedal organ.

The evolution of the pedal organ is a curious chapter in English organ building. First, the solitary bourdon, or 16ft. open; then both, without any separate 8ft.; then when it was realised independent 8ft. tone was desirable, a metal principal or violoncello was supposed to satisfy all a player's needs, and so the average mid-Victorian pedal organ of three stops stood thus: Open diapason, wood 16ft., 30 pipes; bourdon, wood 16ft., 30 pipes; principal or violoncello, metal 8ft., 30 pipes. The general acceptance of this scheme was due to two causes, the amateur-ishness of the organ builder *as an organ player* and the ignorance of the organist as to the possi-bilities of organ construction. The pedal octave came as a makeshift, for of course it doubled in the octave any stops the pedal organ possessed, without allowing the player any individual choice,—no pedal 8ft. being available for separate use, as is so often needed in organ music. Far better than the above scheme—more effective, less costly and taking much less space—was the scheme that succeeded it : open diapason, wood 16ft., 42 pipes ; bourdon, wood 16ft., 42 pipes ; octave, borrowed from open with added top octave ; bass flute, borrowed from bourdon with added top octave. The player then had a choice of using either a stopped or open 8ft. pedal stop, and the full organ gained also in cohesion. This was all the more needful, as most organs had some of their manual foundation stops cut short at tenor C and weakened by grooving into another stop. Often indeed a stopped bass did duty for three 8ft., and this abomination may still be found in many organs.

If to the above pedal is added a violone, it should be borrowed in the same way as a violoncello, and the pedal reed treated in the same manner. One need not be afraid thus to find as many 8ft. as 16ft. on the pedal, for the upper octave may be so graduated and kept down in regulating that there will be in effect no feeling of want of balance; whilst a great sense of firmness and solidity will be imparted to all important pedal passages, at the same time giving the player a great choice as to tone colour and relative power for the beautiful pedal solos which so abound in one of the highest types of organ music, — the Choral Prelude, as found in Bach and in many of the best writers of the day.

Tubular pneumatics, of course, render this borrowing easy and relatively cheap; and, since the tubing may be bent in any direction, the pedal stops can be arranged in the best position for each individual organ, without being bound by the restrictions imposed by tracker work.

Borrowing on the manuals requires very careful

treatment and implies extended sound-boards.   It
is only necessary, in passing, to mention in order
to condemn it, the crude device of making the
tenor   octave   of   a   swell   16ft.   do   double
duty, serving as the bass octave of a diapason,
quite regardless of any differences in tone quality.
This is a species of fraud which seldom fails to
give trouble from the double wind the pipes
receive, and the effect in chords is simply detest-
able, all balance being upset.   Builders have exercised much ingenuity in providing a minimum
number of actual pipes combined with a maximum
amount of mechanism to control them.   There are
undoubtedly cases where, from lack of space, the
matter has been gone into thoroughly and scientifically, the result justifying the means.   One of
the most thoughtful and successful workers in this
direction is, undoubtedly, Mr. Compton, of Not-
tingham, and the following scheme for obtaining
an organ of considerable power and variety out of
nine extended stops of very distinctive character
will make the system clear.   The "collective"
manual, instead of the usual choir, enables the
player to use any of these stops separately or in
combination; but as the pipes themselves cannot
be in two places at the same time, or do double
duty at the same pitch for the hands individually,
such an instrument naturally requires some intim-
acy on the player's part to reveal fully the effects
of which it is capable. Skilfully handled, a listener
would probably think he was listening to an organ
containing thirty or more speaking stops, and the
only fair method of comparison would be to ascertain what stops it would be possible to provide
(preserving, of course, the same quality and standard of work) for an organ costing the same sum,
but built on more conventional lines.

AN ORGAN WITH TWO SWELL CHAMBERS AND NINE ACTUAL OR "PRIMARY" STOPS.

In Swell Chamber No. 1.

(Great Organ.)

1 Large open diapason (FFFF to C⁴)	32ft.	80	pipes
2 Small open diapason (CC to C⁵)	8ft.	73	,,
3 Stopped diapason (CCC to C⁵)	16ft.	85	,,
4 Mixture (two ranks, 12 15)		122	,,
5 Clarinet (CC to C⁴)	8ft.	61	,,

In Swell Chamber No. 2.

(Swell Organ.)

6 Violone (CC to C⁵)	16ft.	85	,,
7 Muted strings (CC to C⁵)	8ft.	232	,,
8 Harmonic flute (CC to C⁶)	8ft.	85	,,
9 Harmonic tromba (CCC to C⁵)	8ft.	85	,,

Here are 908 actual pipes, each of the nine stops carefully chosen so that there are no repetitions of tone quality. An organ of the usual type would consist of two manuals and about eight speaking stops on each and four on the pedals, with the above total number of pipes. Mr. Compton exploits his nine primary stops thus:—

Pedal Organ.

1 Contrabass (to FFFF)	32		6 Violone	... ...	16
1 Contrabass	... ...	16	3 Flute	...	8
3 Bourdon	...	16	9 Trombone ...	...	16

Great Organ.

3 Bourdon	...	16	3 Stopped flute	...	4
1 Large open diapason		8	4 12th and 15th		
2 Small open diapason		8	5 Dbl. clarinet (t.C)		16
3 Stopped diapason ...		8	5 Clarinet	... ...	8
2 Principal	...	4			

Collective Manual.

1	Large open diapason	8	6	Violoncello ...	8
2	Small open diapason	8	7	Muted strings ...	8
3	Stopped diapason ...	8	8	Harmonic flute	8
4	Stopped flute	4	7	Strings	4
5	Double clarinet (t.C)	16	8	Harmonic flute	4
5	Clarinet	8	9	Harmonic tromba	8
6	Violone	16			

Swell Organ.

6	Violone	16	8	Harmonic flute...	4
6	Violoncello	8	8	Harmonic piccolo	2
7	Muted strings	8	9	Contra tromba...	16
8	Harmonic flute ...	8	9	Harmonic tromba	8
6	Viola	4	9	Clarion	4

It has been truly said that the art of combining stops and building up tone is a problem in acoustics, and very curious and interesting results may be thus arrived at synthetically. So the designer comments thus on his own scheme :—

"The swell organ has no open diapason; but a very useful diapason tone may be built up by the combination of violoncello 8ft. and the 8ft. and 4ft. flutes. Moreover, the great organ diapasons, enclosed in their own swell chamber, are usable in many capacities which would otherwise be impossible. The combination of violoncello 8ft. and harmonic flute 4ft. provides a pleasing oboe effect."

Under the name of the "Unit" organ, the late R. Hope-Jones exploited in America this idea of building up a powerful and apparently large organ from a very few extended stops; and in England Messrs. Brindley & Foster have what they term the "metechotic" system. Messrs. Beale & Thynne also, in some of their organs — such as St. John's, Richmond—so arranged their sound-boards that it be-

came possible for the player to draw one or two
reeds, such as the great trumpet, for independent
use on a combined choir and solo manual. But the
further consideration of such interesting schemes
is outside our present object, which is mainly concerned with pointing the way to the improvement
of existing material rather than the construction
of the new, costly and specially planned sound-
boards which are necessary for the success of the
above schemes. In tracker work, nothing could be
done without clumsy complications outweighing
all advantages; in tubular pneumatics, and still
more in electro-pneumatics, the possibilities are
great if we were designing an entirely new instrument. Borrowing has been so abused in a cheap
class of work that it has received a very bad name,
and builders have exercised some ingenuity in in-
venting other names for it, whilst some have
gained much credit for designs which eschew all
"tenor C" work, boldly proclaiming "every stop
goes through," meeting competition in another
way by a very plentiful use of zinc much further
up the scale in the stops than it should ever be
permitted.

It certainly adds much to the expressive capacity of an organ if we are enabled to place both
the solo stop and its accompaniment in a *crescendo*
or *diminuendo* under one operation of the foot, and
this of course becomes practical when any of
the swell stops are duplicated on another manual;
but the additional cost usually stands in the way,
especially in reconstructions.

Some inherent weaknesses of the "extended"
system should be noted. We have seen, in dealing
with scales, that although a good diapason may
be made out of a set of principal pipes by cutting
down and shifting up a few pipes, obtaining
a few more pipes than the bare octave required for the bass, and of course loudening or

softening, &c., to obtain the desired balance. But a principal is not a mere octave diapason of smaller scale; it is intentionally made brighter and louder in tone to give the necessary firmness and ring to the entire organ. The extension, if applied to these two stops, cannot therefore give the same results; there will probably be effected a compromise which injures both stops. Next, if a full chord be played by the left hand and duplicated an octave higher by the right (all the stops being drawn) several of the pipes already sounded by the left hand cannot do duty again to reinforce the right, and it requires exceptional skill so to arrange matters that this weakness shall not be too apparent.

Balance of Tone.

THE ill-balanced church organ consisting of an inferior pedal organ of one or two 16ft. stops only (with no 8ft. tone to give firmness), a starved "great" and a swell of about twice as many stops as the great, one can only mention to condemn. Just as faulty in principle is the sketchy three-manual, in which over a feeble pedal department we find a great and swell reduced to five or six stops each in order to get a choir of four or five.

Even the smallest two-manual organ should have for its pedal a bourdon and a bass flute, the latter of course derived from the bourdon with an additional top octave. The small space required for these little extra pipes and the small extra amount of tubing, &c., needed are of slight consideration in regard to the general usefulness of the 8ft. stop. This is the normal pedal for a small church organ with from four to six stops each on great and swell.

The next step is an important one,— the addition of a 16ft. open, with an 8ft. open derived in the same way from it, forming a four-stop pedal for great and swell manuals up to ten stops on each. But when height and space are strictly limited, there is an alternative scheme, which has sometimes been adopted. A 16ft. pedal reed, if of mitred or half-length tubes, may be placed in many positions where an open 16ft. would be quite impossible; and, if smoothly and carefully voiced, will give great richness and dignity even to a small organ. Messrs. Walker have done this at Welbeck Abbey (1893), the pedal consisting of bourdon 16ft. (with extension for an octave pedal) and contra fagotto 16ft., as the foundation for a great of five stops (8ft., 8ft., 8ft., 4ft., 4ft.) and a swell of six (8ft., 8ft., 8ft., 8ft., 4ft., 8ft.).

In the building up of tone on the great organ long experience has proved that against three flue stops of 8ft. pitch we require: one of 16ft. (either stopped or open), two of 4ft. (a principal and a flute), one of 2ft., one of $2\frac{2}{3}$ft. (twelfth), and a mixture of three or four ranks, with an 8ft. trumpet as the most important reed, in order to obtain a due proportion of fulness and brilliance of tone. If the organ has a third manual, the two opens (which should be of good, heavy metal, boldly voiced, yet differing in quality and power) and a full-toned wald flute or clarabella of wood will give a sufficient body of 8ft. tone; a great sound-board of these ten stops sufficing for most churches seating from 500 to 1000 people. But in the case of a two-manual, another metal 8ft., a soft stop of the dulciana type, is absolutely necessary in addition, for we must have something suitable as an accompaniment to a solo on one of the swell stops, and cannot cripple our "great" by reducing one of its three 8ft. for that purpose. The clarinet, too, will have to be on the great sound-board, so that while we may regard a ten-stop sound-board as a "complete" one for a three-manual instrument, one of twelve slides is required for a two-manual.

Very large churches do not concern us here; they will, of course, require more, but these additions are practically duplications which merely carry on the general principles here laid down. The one chorus reed of 8ft. will be enriched by a 16ft. reed for depth and fulness of tone, and by a 4ft. clarion for brilliance, and the mixture ranks increased.

In the above ten-stop great the chorus reed requires to balance it on the pedals, the addition of a 16ft. reed, using full length tubes; wooden tubes being mostly preferred for the bottom octave. And it might also with great advantage be borrowed at octave pitch as an independent 8ft. stop far more frequently than is usually done. We then have a really firm and dignified pedal of six stops, derived from three sets of pipes, 42 in each set.

The Acoustic Bass, or Quint.

MANY specifications include this stop in a pedal organ of four or five stops only. I have even met with it as one of the three: open 16ft., bourdon 16ft., and quint, where it certainly thickened the pedal, but at the expense of clearness. It is, of course, a mere substitute for the very costly 32ft. open. As there are examples which are satisfactory, the best means of obtaining the result must here be briefly described. The bourdon is borrowed for its lower octave and a half, the CCC pipe speaking at CC, and so on, and an octave of stopped quints (GG to G) provided for the lowest octave of the pedals. These, if the voicing is soft and pure, and the acoustic conditions favourable, create the illusion of a 32ft. tone speaking on the bottom octave, whilst the bourdon is in actual 32ft. pitch for the upper one-and-a-half octaves of the pedal board.

Stopped pipes carried down to CCC, 32ft. pitch, are generally most unsatisfactory; but they can be taken down to the limit of the vocal compass (FFFF) with good results, and it is worth doing when circumstances permit. The pipes at $10\frac{2}{3}$ft. (GG to G) are sometimes borrowed also from the bourdon, so that the acoustic or harmonic bass has not a single pipe of its own; but the quint cannot then be subordinate to the real pitch as it should be.

The Contra Bass, or Violone.

THERE are many excellent examples of this pedal stop which give a very good representation of the "bite" or attack of the bow on the double bass; and, as the scale is considerably less than that of the usual English open diapason of 16ft., it might in certain cases appear in its stead with the advantage of saving space. The scale of examples by Schülze (in wood) were 5¾ inches square, by Lewis (in zinc) 6 inches in diameter, and the tone quality depends to a great extent on the pipes being bearded.

The Echo Bourdon.

THE usefulness of a very quiet 16ft. bass for one or two of the softest stops was recognised by the old builders before the days of tubular pneumatics, when they divided the swell double so that the lower twelve notes might be drawn separately,—a very crude makeshift. But in modern work it is well worth the extra cost to add the swell bourdon to our pedal sound-board by tubular connection. Attempts have also been made to use the pedal bourdon in two gradations of tone by cutting the wind supply, which of course slightly flattens the pitch at the same time, though not very appreciably in the lower octave.

Characteristic Tone on the Pedals.

BUILDERS have not yet got out of the habit of regarding the pedal organ as merely supplying a bass without any very definite ideas as to tone-quality, although we never regard the bass instruments of an orchestra in this light. Anyone who has access to a good organ possessing a really well voiced and rich toned 8ft. octave to the clarinet instead of an incomplete specimen ending with tenor C will be able to realise what a valuable addition it would be to any organ if carried down to 16ft. pitch as a bass clarinet on the pedals. There is no reason why it should be made a very expensive item even in a small organ, for the tubes being straight and of short length and small scale would occupy much less in ground space and height than any other 16ft. stop. As an alternative to the Walker scheme I have quoted, it could be used with excellent results by a good voicer, and even a small organ might thus possess a firm and decisive pedal with some character. In larger instruments having a full scale and powerful trombone of full length tubes, it would also be useful as affording a great contrast in tone, quality and relative power. A viole d'orchestre could also be treated in the same way at 16ft. pitch if in the hands of voicers who know how to preserve the characteristic quality of tone without slow speech. The narrow scale wooden violone would probably always be preferred; the metal 16ft. viol is only suggested in cases where it would be difficult to find space for a 6in. scale of wood. In the best types of organ music, pedal passages of melodic importance abound, and we ought to have the means wherewith to render them with the quality as well as power of tone they demand, without the clumsy expedient of coupling to a manual we would rather leave free for some other tone colour or combination.

Blowing.

A FIRM, ample wind supply is most essential to every organ, and a few hints about it have already been given in the Introduction. The various means whereby steadiness is secured may now be considered. If the reader will examine any ordinary bellows, he will notice two pairs of ribs, divided by a middle-board; one pair opening inwardly and the other outwardly, thus affording compensation under all conditions with respect to the pressure, or compression of air, by this inversion. Counterbalances (strips of iron) are screwed to upper, middle and lower-boards in such a way as to ensure the correct level as the bellows rise. There may also be a concussion valve (though it is not absolutely indispensable when all the other conditions are fulfilled). It is a small feeder attached to the wind trunk, controlled by a stout spring, and in the event of any sudden jerkiness it steadies the flow of wind automatically, being in effect a "give and take" arrangement in relation to pressure. To prevent the bellows becoming unduly distended (75 degrees is the usual limit), there is a small waste pallet, controlled by a strong cord, to let the excess of wind out. This is sometimes made to open at the top of the bellows, but should always be made to do so internally. The feeders are the two diagonal shaped bellows which, opening and closing alternately, compress the air within the reservoir portion of the bellows. The weights regulating the wind pressure should be of cast iron, in slabs of about an inch in thickness, neatly arranged around the edges of the top-board, and screwed in to prevent accidental shifting when once they are correctly distributed so that the bellows rise and fall always at the same level. Or, as preferred by many modern builders, stout spiral springs may be placed at the corners, and the final regulation of the desired wind pressure be adjusted by wind gauge with the help of a small weight or two only.

But all the above means are still insufficient to secure absolute steadiness under all conditions. In the best work the bellows delivers its wind into a separate reservoir for at least one of the manuals ; and even in organs of only two manuals, a builder of the first rank will justly deem it necessary for the reputation of his work to place such a reservoir underneath the swell sound-board.

A severe test for steadiness, whereby the player may test for himself in various organs—good, bad and indifferent—whether ill-timed economies have been practised with regard to the wind supply, would be as follows: Draw all the stops, holding down a full chord with the right hand, and play the same chord staccato with the left hand and pedals. If in the interval a tremulousness is imparted to the notes held by the right hand, something has evidently been sacrificed to cheapness. Herein lies one of the most important points of difference in price shown in builders' estimates for

organs apparently similar in size, general design
and specified materials.

It should be stated that one cause of possible
unsteadiness must not be overlooked when applying this test: a crowded sound-board with shallow
grooves and well, and small wind trunks, will also
create it. The bellows handle must be correctly
levered, and well lubricated with grease; but must
not "spring" (i.e., move an inch or so before it
begins to raise the feeders), but should be perfectly
rigid, and made of birch, not pitch pine.

Before the days of mechanical blowing, Conti-
nental organs had a much superior arrangement
to the bellows handle common with us. Half-a-
dozen simple feeders would each be controlled by
planks of wood, and all the blower had to do was
to step on one of these, holding on to a handrail;
and, as it slowly sank a foot or so with his weight,
he simply passed on to the next, watching the slow
rise of each feeder belonging to the various departments of the organ. Many years ago the writer
had thus blown a Silbermann organ, with six pedal
stops (including a 32ft. open), for a fellow student,
with no more sense of fatigue than if one had been
walking about the church. But all these organs
were on light wind pressures; probably not more
than $2\frac{1}{2}$in. or $2\frac{5}{8}$in. being the equivalent as we
estimate pressure, and, of course, if applied to the
pressures now in use, the blower would have to
supply himself with weights like a diver.

Probably the bellows handle will always exist,
as a quaint survival, in out of the way places
where neither water, gas or electricity is available.
But players thus dependent on human aid are
much to be commiserated: playing is certainly
robbed of half its pleasure. Petrol engines have
been tried, but are presumably not very successful;
at any rate, they are not much in evidence, and the
mechanical genius who will abolish the bellows

handle for good and all will deserve knight-hood at least.

We have now to consider the relative claims of the three motive forces used in blowing.

HYDRAULIC ENGINES.

This, the oldest motive power employed, is still the safest and most reliable (though not always the most economical) where all the conditions are favourable. A high pressure must be available, even in times of drought, and it must not be liable to be cut off or run short in summer. About 40lbs. to the square inch may be reckoned a low pressure, about 20lbs. being an absolute minimum for even a small chamber organ on a light wind. Wherever severe frost is expected each winter, water power is at a great disadvantage; still, ways and means may be found in many cases of minimising this drawback. The shafting is easily attached direct to the bellows handle, and can be made to discon-nect instantaneously for hand blowing in case of emergency. For the rest, having secured from the local water company a guarantee as to the pres-sure when at its lowest (this should be tested and not allowed to rest on guess work), the reader has but to communicate with some of the makers advertising in the musical papers when, on filling up a simple form stating the number of strokes of the bellows handle required per minute to sustain a full chord on the full organ, the size, horse power and price, &c., are easily determined.

GAS ENGINES.

Before the present abnormal rise in the price of gas, its use for blowing purposes had cer-tainly the recommendation of cheapness for large organs wherever the price of gas was fairly low.

Before the war (which has trebled the cost of gas) large towns were supplied at about 2s. 6d. per thousand feet, and quite a large organ could be blown at this rate for about threepence or fourpence per hour. But the disadvantages are considerable. A gas engine cannot be started instantaneously, like the hydraulic engine or electric motor; a wheel has first to be set in motion after firing up, and this is a messy and tiresome operation at best. More serious, however, is the difficulty of preventing the gas fumes from being drawn with the current of air into the organ and creating a nauseating effect at the console. Many organs have had the tongues of the reeds quite ruined by corrosion from gas fumes, and altogether this method is only to be recommended when water power or electricity is not available.

ELECTRIC MOTORS.

These, properly installed, are reliable and efficient. The numerous makes of fans on the market testify to their ever increasing popularity. The force generated by quite small fans is enormous, and they are now usually and preferably coupled direct to the electric motor instead of to countershafting, thus avoiding the trouble incidental to the use of belts and also economising in power. Feeders are no longer needed; a trunk, usually about 9in. in diameter, leading directly into the reservoirs will give a perfectly steady and ample wind; and, if the right horse power motor is applied, the reservoirs will only drop about two inches when a sustained chord is played on the full organ. Fan blowing is, in fact, a perfect godsend to many organs which, on any other system, would be deplorably short winded and unsteady. Silencing arrangements, as well as efficient starting switches, have long since been perfected by all the best makers, so that the obsolete or defective examples of blowing by electricity which may occasionally be met with need create no prejudice. Before the present great rise in the price of current, a three-manual organ with about thirty speaking stops, requiring a motor of from two to three horse power, could be blown for about fourpence per hour, or even less where a large demand for power purposes enabled the electricity companies to supply at a cheap rate of about three-halfpence or twopence per unit.

Small two-manual organs can be quite successfully blown by gearing the bellows handle to a small motor, at an expenditure of only one unit or less in current, costing much less per hour than hand labour. A rotary movement has been applied to the motor also with successful results, the motor causing a wheel tyred like that of a bicycle to revolve, with suitable gearing in connection with the bellows handle. As local conditions vary so much, the reader must pursue his investigations with an open mind, and only a few hints of a general nature can be given here.

General Arrangements and Position.

IT is a great gain to the wellbeing of any organ when it is so designed that every part of it may be got at with the least delay to rectify a fault; and the attention of builders may well be directed to the following points:—

1. The desk and panels should be arranged to lift out, without being screwed in.

2. In a three manual organ, preference to be given to a form of action which enables the two upper key-frames to be lifted out instantly. In small two-manual organs, this is not perhaps quite so essential for easy access to each part of the action, and many builders use a form of action in which stickers pass through the tail ends of the swell keys.

3. Fixed steps to be provided to the main passage board, which should be at least fifteen or sixteen inches wide. In many organs a stout tuner is a serious danger, and acrobatic feats are apparently expected at times by those who plan organs.

4. Mixtures are often so buried behind reeds and other larger stops in a swell box that it becomes quite a risky operation to reach them at all for tuning. Reeds are also often too crowded, so that the farthest set — there should never be more than three together—can scarcely be reached without disturbing the tuning wires of another set.

5. Instead of securing the front-boards of soundboards with many screws, the French plan of using some form of wedge is preferable, saving much time when dealing with a faulty pallet or its spring.

6. In fairly large swell boxes, when practicable, there should be a door in one of the sides or at the back, or a removable panel. Whether passages are provided down the centre of large sound-boards or across them, will depend, of course, upon the shape of the organ site and the number of stops on the sound-board.

7. An ideal arrangement to facilitate access to the intricate mechanism that a large organ contains and to add enormously to the resonance of the whole organ would be to expect of future architects that they provide an adjoining chamber for the main bellows and all the blowing arrangements; it should, of course, be kept at the same temperature as the church. It might also be made to serve as a convenient library for the choir music.

It is desirable that, wherever possible, great, swell and choir sound-boards should be on the same level, so that all the metal pipes may be subjected to the same temperature. And in tracker work especially, depth is a great consideration, so that choir and swell may be placed immediately behind the great. We have then a "straight action," and awkward complications are avoided. If the depth is insufficient for great, choir and swell to be thus placed in line, the choir *may* be taken off at right angles with a horizontal roller-board under the swell box in tracker work; and, though liability to cipher is somewhat increased, it is yet probably to be preferred to having two kinds of touch in the same instrument. Each church will present some feature of its own to take into account, the problem being to allow as much of the tone of the organ *as a whole* to reach the congregation without being obstructed.

In the usual chancel position, with its almost inevitable organ chamber having one large arch opening into the chancel and a smaller one facing down the church, the mistake is often made of placing the pedal organ in this latter position. Apart from the fact that large wood pipes do not lend themselves well to decorative treatment, all those occupying seats in the immediate neighbourhood will hear a great deal too much of the unsubdued power of the pedal organ, to the detriment of the more delicate stops, unless there exists a very considerable space between.

One often remembers with regret the glorious effect of organ tone proceeding from a roomy west end gallery; but we have here to make the best of things as they are, and the following sketches suggest three different methods of dealing with the usual chancel position:—

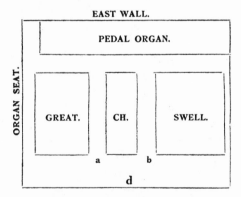

Here the larger pedal pipes would be stayed against the wall, the smaller in front of them, with long feet wherever desirable, to prevent any blocking of the mouths of those at the back. A good wide passage way is also desirable in front of the pedal organ, and good roomy passage boards at (*a*) and (*b*), not only for the purposes of tuning, but to provide clear open spaces for the tone of the pedal organ to come well through and blend with the manual tone so that the whole may be reflected together by the two walls of the chancel through each opening. (*d*) is a door giving access both to the organ and the organist's seat, and the corner between might most profitably be occupied by a substantial book-case enabling the organist to keep his music in proper condition, a matter our church architects never by any chance think of making provision for.

But the chamber may be too shallow to allow the three manual sound-boards to be thus placed in line with the direct action a builder would naturally prefer.

To meet such cases this alternative is suggested:—

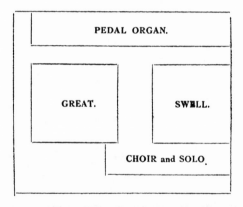

Here the swell box is shown built against the wall, and the third manual might be made a combined choir and solo organ. If so, and the space permitted, it could be enclosed in a small swell box of its own, the side of the larger swell box forming the back. Or the clarinet only (which should on no account be deprived of its bottom octave, as is so frequently the case) might be placed in the swell box. Should there be a second reed, an orchestral oboe would be the best choice as a good contrast. Each case presents its own special conditions; in some chambers another swell box, however small, would be undesirable, and there is also a certain charm in the unen - closed tone of a few tranquil accompanimental stops floating away freely into the church.

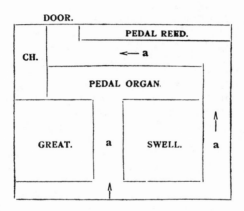

Still adhering to the principle of allowing as much of the tone as a whole to reach the congregation and choir, our third ground plan allows for a door at the east end, with an ample passage way, which should not be less than two feet, at the back of the organ, leading to it. The choir organ (which must now, of course, be tubular pneumatic) may also have a passage way underneath it into the chancel. Or, if the depth is sufficient, the pedal organ, or a part of it, may be placed against the south wall. But it would probably be better to give as much space as possible between great and swell to let the tone come through. Such space is by no means wasted; a healthy clearness results from allowing the mingled voices of the full organ to gather and focus themselves, if one may so express it, before expulsion into the church. In this third arrangement the tubing for the pedal reed is simply bunched together and passed under the floor; the pedal opens with plenty of space wherein to speak across the passage way, with the bourdons at their back. These do not so much mind being crowded, and are always at their best with their backs against a wall or against another set of large wood pipes. To avoid the sympathy engendered by the semi-tonal arrangement of bourdons, builders often prefer placing their metal principals or violoncellos in alternation with the bourdons, when not required for the front. They are sometimes displayed in this way in the case work, but the effect is not pleasing to the eye. For access to the passage boards steps should be provided; the bellows and action being protected by neat panelling, not screwed up, but fitted so as to move easily or slide in a groove for free, instantaneous access to every part. In a west end position the plan is usually quite simple; great, choir and swell in line, the pedal organ divided to form the sides of the case, or placed at the back, which is generally preferable in effect. Occasionally the site is so shallow that great and swell have to be arranged side by side. To preserve a window, the organ is sometimes divided, with the console between, but although it may not be bad acoustically, the effect is not dignified. Antiphonal effects from much divided organs, although at first the novelty may please, usually end in distracting the attention needlessly, and the best results are obtained when the sound is diffused most equally over every part of the building. If the organ is to be divided, its main body of tone — great, swell and pedal —

should be concentrated as much as possible, leaving choir and solo for the opposite side.

Many architects are notoriously unsympathetic towards the requirements of the modern organ, and churches with transepts and their peaked roofs at right angles to the nave and chancel are especially bad for intercepting and confusing the sound-waves. Such a roof over an organ causes a din about the player's ears, giving a very unpleasant impression of even a good organ, and builders have sometimes very wisely (if they have a reputation to lose) simply declined to tender for a position wherein an organ could do them no credit. But sometimes the fault does not rest with the architect, and a glaring instance occurs in a certain London suburb. Here the architect had provided ample space behind the decani stalls for an organ of suitable proportions, with plenty of space overhead and no obstructions whatever to the tone on either side. But the "powers that be" (although the church was quite large enough for the congregation attending it), decided to obtain more ground space, and the organ was placed overhead with a detached console below. And the only means of rectifying the smallest defect in that organ is by placing a tall ladder against the front, removing one or two of the front pipes and clambering in and out at some risk to one's neck. On the ground floor, the organ would have had an excellent effect; but, thus skied, the height above the pipes is insufficient and the effect is very disappointing, as might have been foreseen.

The Organ Front.

THIS should slightly overhang the player, the curved "ogee" form, or a central tower of pipes, presenting an appearance at once more graceful and dignified than a straight line or flat of pipes. This overhang ought never to exceed two feet, for the player must not be buried beneath his instrument, or condemned to the perpetual use of artificial light. The overhang saves him from being subjected to the full force of the great organ; in excess it prevents him from judging accurately a correct balance in his accompaniment.

The "reversed console" was attempted occasionally in tracker work before the invention of tubular pneumatics; if deemed desirable, it would be best whenever space can be allowed on the opposite side of the chancel to place the console there,—of course, facing the organ. Better still it is for the accompanist when he can be placed above and in full view of the choir, with the voices rising up to him,—a possibility only in very lofty chancels.

The leading English builders have issued many elaborate books of designs for fronts: many of them excellent, many also containing remarkable examples of what to avoid. One of the most irritating eyesores (because architecturally false in principle) is frequently shown in American organ builders' designs,—long flats of pipes of the same scale, all cut to the same length, thus revealing themselves to be dummies, without even the pretence of following any natural law.

In west end positions, especially in the north of England, may be seen many straight, stiff and curious designs in which rostrum and console, and sometimes the Communion table are mixed up. Another fault consists in tamely filling up an arch with a semi-circular row of pipes, mostly dummies, exactly following the curve of the arch instead of grouping them, so as to stand out boldly against it. An over-elaboration of case work, showing several flats of small pipes, is a feature in many old organs. At Perpignan, in the Pyrenées Orientales, a central feature is a flat of small pipes *upside down*, apparently intended to suggest a reflection of a similar group beneath them. It may be seen in Töpfer, plate xlvii., fig. 7.

The student of design will find thirty-two interesting photo reproductions of good English case work in the "Dictionary of Organs and Organists," published by Messrs. Logan of Bournemouth. The reader is advised to study them well, with an eye to their relative appropriateness to the particular situation in which he may be interested.

As to decoration, the silvering or aluminium paint treatment now so much in evidence has a good deal to recommend it, especially in connection with light oak. It brightens many an otherwise dark corner in a church. The old practice of gilding, although temporarily out of fashion, really has a fine effect with dark oak; and it will probably come into its own again and banish much of the cheap and hideous diapering which makes the organ a positive eyesore in many churches. Good spotted metal, of course, needs no adornment; but it has already been stated that we do not get the same weight of tone from it when used for the 8ft. great open diapason basses, which are mostly required for the case, though it is, of course, infinitely to be preferred to zinc for tone and appearance. Pitchpine is altogether too prevalent in the cheap modern organ, and presents a very undignified and vulgar appearance. Plain deal, properly stained and varnished or painted, may be made to look quite well. The one essential point to observe is, however, that the woodwork and the whole design must harmonise with its surroundings.

The Ideal Organ.

TO attain this, a "combination of the talents," mechanical and tonal, would be necessary, together with the following conditions :—

1. A large and lofty church, with perfect acoustics and a fine position for the organ.

2. A carefully thought-out scheme, specifying in detail the particular material known and proved to be the best for its special purpose in every part of its structure.

3. A good deal of the voicing and all the regulating and experimenting with various tonal combinations to be done in the church, ample funds being held in hand to allow for this.

The ideal organ will not be one of a hundred stops or more but of about half that number, well chosen and perfectly placed on fine roomy soundboards; for it must, in its fullest power, remain essentially a *musical* instrument, and our eardrums must not be smitten and stunned with such overwhelming power that the capacity for enjoying the most delicate qualities of tone is temporarily destroyed.

These conditions realised, the result would be superior to any attempted scheme on paper,—such as is only heard in dreams.

New Methods of Tone Production.

DOUBLE LANGUID PIPES.

I N patents of 1909, Mr. Vincent Willis, the inventor to whom English organ building owes so much, worked out an entirely new treatment of organ pipes, which I give in his own words :—

This invention relates to the pipework of the organ and to the method or means employed to supply "flue" pipes with air under pressure. The invention is an attempt to enable the organ builder to obtain, when necessary, diapason or other tones found in the organ in greater power or volume than heretofore and without the deterioration or change in quality of tone which attends, and therefore limits, increase of volume of sound by ordinary methods. But the invention is also useful when a higher development of overtones is sought without an increase of tonal output.

Of two similarly voiced "flue" pipes of the diapason type, for instance, speaking the same note and of appropriate but different scales, the trained ear will, on the question of quality of tone only, prefer the pipe of smaller scale, because it is naturally richer in overtones. By the application of this invention to the larger scale pipe a development of overtones similar to, or, if desired, higher than that found in the smaller scale pipe can be obtained in the greater volume of sound of the larger scale pipe; in other words the control of scale over quality of tone has been reduced.

The speaking lengths of two such pipes differ, the smaller scale pipe being the longer of the two. This difference in length would appear to be due to the greater velocity of the air in the smaller scale pipe. In reed pipes however this condition is reversed, the large scale pipe being the longer of the two.

Therefore in the case of flue pipes requiring the aid of this invention, I accelerate the velocity of the air in the pipe; and in the case of reed pipes I retard the velocity of the air.

To apply the invention to a flue pipe made of metal, I fit the pipe rigidly or moveably with an upper or false langward,* making the space between the front edges of the two langwards that of a wide flue or, for special purposes, very much greater. I prefer to part the langwards at the back sufficiently to permit of a perforation of the back of the pipe between the langwards when necessary. I prefer also to make the langward proper thinner than usual, or to invert it, and to make the front edge of the upper langward, which should be slightly set back, thin enough to be suitably treated and adjusted by the voicer; but the two langwards might be combined in one casting. It will now be seen that the stream of air from the flue of the pipe, rushing past the opening between the two langwards, creates suction in the cavity between the langwards. If (1) the back of the pipe between the langwards be perforated, external air in a volume determined by the size of the perforation will be drawn through the cavity to unite with, and to increase the volume of, the stream of air from the flue of the pipe. If (2) the upper or false langward be perforated, air will be drawn from the body of the pipe, with a like result as to the volume of the stream of air from the flue of the pipe. If (3) the langward proper be perforated, air under pressure will be admitted to the cavity, also with a like result as to the volume of the stream of air from the flue.

In the first and third cases, the stream of air from the flue will be deflected outwardly and an increased velocity of the stream of air from the flue of the pipe will produce a correspondingly increased deflecting effort. The voicer is thereby provided with a powerful means of neutralising the tendency of a pipe to attempt harmonic utterance when forced. In the second case the stream is first deflected outwardly as in the other cases; but the indraught at the upper part of the mouth is now increased, the net result being an inward deflection of the stream of air.

By one or other of these methods or by a combination of the first and second methods, increased tonal output with the desired development of overtones can be obtained from any class of

---

* "Languid," "language," "langward,"—the flat metal plate at the top of the foot has been thus variously termed.

metal flue pipe. The first arrangement may be applied to large scale open pipes with thick, rounded, bearded or leathered lips, and to harmonic pipes. The second arrangement is peculiarly adapted to stopped pipes. The third method, requiring air under pressure, is not economical but may be valuable as a means of controlling the utterance of very large open pipes.

Stops imitative of string tones can already be produced in very great perfection by the aid of the roller beard now some sixty or seventy years old. But the tonal output of the upper part of stops of this class has usually to be somewhat restricted because the utterance and tone of certain pipes, which are generally found in two or three groups of two or three successive notes, cannot be brought up to the standard of others, and these pipes have to be "faked" rather than voiced. This difficulty, which is generally attributed to a faulty construction of pipe, is in reality due to disturbing vibrations of the air in the foot of the pipe or in the windway leading to the foot of the pipe. Nor is the improved construction of pipe described above free from this influence when bearded.

Before, therefore, the greatest tonal output and the highest development of overtones can be obtained throughout these stops, all adverse conditions must be removed.

The obvious remedy for vibratory disturbance from the air in the foot of the pipe is to alter the length of the foot either by shortening it or by lengthening it with a boot.

But this treatment does not avail when the disturbing vibrations are in the windway leading to the foot. A pipe may speak well over one "wind" and badly over another. In the case of flue pipes, this difficulty can be entirely removed. If, instead of the ordinary method of supplying the pipe with air under pressure, one or more jets of air, at a suitable pressure, are employed as an injector, the necessary pressure at the flue of the pipe can be obtained with the foot open to free air, and any vibratory impulses set up at the flue of the pipe can travel harmlessly down the foot into free air. If, in practice, the noise of the injector can be sufficiently muffled by the use of absorbent materials or by other silencing treatment, this method of supplying flue pipes with air under pressure may completely supersede the present system.

The principle of this invention is equally applicable to flue pipes made of wood, the different material necessitating, of course, different methods of construction. The false langward or block, taking any one of the forms common to the blocks of wooden pipes, may now be of some thickness and may be also fitted with a loose facing of wood or metal for adjustment and treatment by the voicer. This false block may be either built into the pipe or made adjustable by means of a screw through the back of the pipe. With the ordinary form of mouth, it is necessary to mount the cap on a loose facing like that of a Vienna flute. With the inverted form of mouth, this facing is not absolutely necessary.

Where the highest results are sought, and cost is not a consideration, an adjustable upper lip gives the voicer the same power over a wooden pipe as he has over a metal one, and greatly facilitates the application of roller or other beards to wooden pipes.

If the loose facing of the adjustable false block be suitably shaped, it may be made to act as an internal roller beard and an open pipe can then speak under inverted conditions,—that is to say, almost all the wind from the flue, together with that drawn in through the perforation described more particularly in connection with metal flue pipes, passing up the pipe instead of, as normally, outside it. But in this example the air drawn in through the perforation is only equivalent to the air which would be drawn in past the ordinary external roller beard, and there is therefore no advantage in this arrangement.

The remarks as to the methods and effects of applying the invention to metal flue pipes hold true for flue pipes of wood, and need not, therefore, be repeated here.

To apply this invention to reed pipes in which a higher development of the overtones is required, I attach a plate to the head of the reed or shallot, allowing it to project over the head of the reed far enough to prevent air from rushing in between the tongue and the head of the reed. This plate or baffle may be attached to the head of the reed by a rivet or screw in order that it may be turned out of the way whilst the face of the reed is being surfaced. By limiting the inrush of compressed air into the reed or shallot, this contrivance reduces the pressure therein, prevents choking, and consequently ensures a better utilisation of the energy of the compressed air on the tongue. The baffle may be continued round the sides of the tongue for a little distance and with some advantage, but, practically, the simple plate is all that is necessary.

In cases where it is desired to emphasize the ground tone and overtones of the pipe equally, I remove the head of the reed from its usual position and, without altering the reed itself, I fit the head in a position further up the reed at a distance from its usual position not exceeding one-sixth or one-fifth the tuning length of the tongue. A very practical way of carrying out this treatment in small reeds is to make the head somewhat thicker than usual and to trench or groove it from the outside to the required width and depth.

By so placing the head of the reed, I ensure a longer closing of the opening, a reduced influx of air, a longer period between the influxes, and consequently an equal intensification of ground tone and overtones.

Figs. 1 and 2 of the drawings are sections showing a method of applying this invention to flue pipes constructed of metal.

Figs. 3 and 4 are sections showing methods of applying this invention to flue pipes constructed of wood.

Fig. 5 is a section showing means by which the utterance of flue pipes may be freed from inimical vibrations originating in the air in the foot of the pipe or in the windway leading to the foot.

Fig. 6 is a section, and

Fig. 7 is an end view, showing a method of adapting this invention to reed pipes.

Fig. 8 is a front view showing an application of this invention to reed pipes.

In Fig. 1, (A) is the foot, and (B) the body, of an open flue pipe constructed of metal; (a) is the langward proper: (b) the false langward; (c) the cavity or space between the langwards; (a²) the flue of the pipe; (b²) the opening between the two langwards, or the false flue; (c) the perforation in the back of the pipe.

The stream of air from the flue of the pipe (a²), rushing past the false flue (b²), draws in free air through the opening (c) as shown by the arrow. The reinforced stream impinges on the lip of the pipe, a greater quantity of air than usual passing up the pipe, with the result that the pipe speaks with an unusually high development of overtones.

In Fig. 2 (A) is the foot, and (B) the body, of a stopped or partially stopped flue pipe constructed of metal; (a) is the langward proper; (b) the false langward, which is turned up at the back of the pipe in order to establish communication between the air in the cavity (c) and that in the body of the pipe (B), and also to avoid an angle of inert air; (a²) is the flue of the pipe; (b²) the opening between the two langwards, or the false flue.

The stream of air from the flue of the pipe (a²), rushing past the false flue (b²), draws in air from the body of the pipe (B), as shown by the arrow. The reinforced stream of air impinges on the lip of the pipe, none, of course, passing up the pipe; but greater variations of density in the air of the body of the pipe are obtained than heretofore, and consequently there is a higher development of overtones.

In Fig. 3, (A) is the foot, and (B) the body, of an open flue pipe constructed of wood; (a) is the block proper; (b) the false block, which is fitted with a removable facing of wood or metal (b³); (c) is the space between the blocks; (a²) the flue of the pipe; (b²) the false flue; (c) the perforation in the back of the pipe. To provide for access to the removable facing (b³), it is necessary to mount the cap (d) on a removable facing (e).

The stream of air from the flue (a²) draws in free air through the opening (c), as described in reference to Fig. 1, and with like results.

In Fig. 4, (A) is the foot, and (B) the body, of a stopped or partially stopped flue pipe constructed of wood; (a) is the block

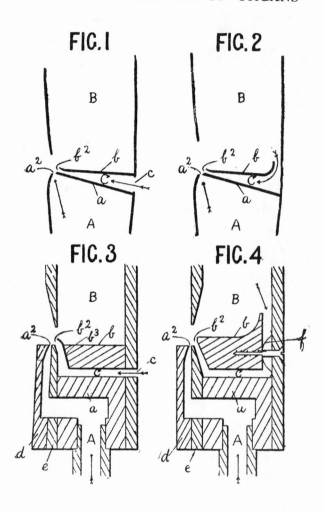

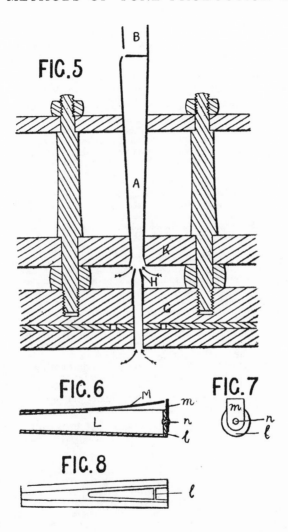

FIC.5

FIC.6

FIC.7

FIC.8

proper; (*b*) the false block, which may be made adjustable by means of a screw through the back of the pipe acting against a spring such as (*f*); (c) is the space between the blocks; (*a*²) the flue of the pipe; (*b*²) the false flue; the cap (*d*) is mounted on the removable facing (*e*).

The stream of air from the flue of the pipe (*a*²) draws in air through the passage (c) from the body of the pipe (B), as described in reference to Fig. 2, and with like results.

I believe the late M. Cavaillé-Coll's theory of the speech of a flue pipe, which regards the stream of air from the flue as an aerial tongue, is generally accepted. But a rough investigation of the speech of flue pipes constructed as described above points to more complicated aerial movements: therefore the details shown in the drawings must be regarded as variable and suggestive.

In Fig. 5, (G) is an upper board of a sound-board of ordinary construction which, instead of receiving the foot of a pipe in the usual manner, is fitted with a nozzle (H). Above the upper board (G) is arranged a second upper-board (K), which may be supported at a suitable height by distance pieces or blank nuts, the ordinary rack pillars being lengthened as shown, in order to permit of this arrangement. The foot of the pipe, instead of resting in a countersink in the usual manner, is fitted into the upper-board (K) as shown. A jet of air passing through the nozzle (H) at a suitable pressure can act as an injector, drawing in free air as shown by the arrows, and forcing it into the foot of the pipe (A). The final regulation of a stop of pipes would be accomplished by reducing or enlarging the nozzles by proper tools as small pipes are tuned.

In Figs. 6 and 7, (L) is the body of a reed of ordinary construction, (*l*) being the head of the reed; (M) is the tongue; (*m*) the baffle, attached to the head by the rivet (*n*).

Fig. 8 shows the head of a reed (*l*) in its new position.

The baffle (*m*) on Figs. 6 and 7 limits the influx of compressed air without lengthening the period between the influxes. The removed head of Fig. 8 reduces the influx of compressed air and lengthens the period between the influxes.

Commenting on these double languid pipes, Mr. Duprey, whom I have previously quoted concerning mixtures, observes :—

"It is now possible to produce a volume of tone and richness of quality undreamt of previously, with the most incisive and clean cut articulation and repetition, without which the modern orchestral player is helpless. The forced single languid, widemouthed diapasons of Schülze and his followers were certainly very fine. But the attack was poor and the speech unsteady. They held their own for a time, until purely organ music ceased to be the chief item on the recital organist's programme. Any attempt to gain rapidity of speech by softening the pipe immediately destroyed the tone quality. In short, the tone was there when you got it. Now that the full tone is to be had at the moment of speech, as from a drum, and in enormous volume besides, the organ pipe is placed on another footing."

PIPES SPEAKING IN ATTENUATED AIR.

Another patent, accepted 1913, runs as follows :

This invention relates to organs or to parts of an organ from which the tonal output need not be large; chamber organs, for example, or echo and celestial organs, which are often with advantage located at a distance from the main organ.

The primary object of the invention is the production of an instrument better adapted in construction to the average room than the ordinary organ.

With this object I employ attenuated air, as with the free reed in the American organ, enclosing the pipe work in an airtight box constructed in such a manner as to transmit as far as practicable the sound from the pipes, and also in a second and outer box, constructed to operate as an ordinary swell box, to shut in or let out sound as required.

The ready response of the drum head to sound waves or vibrations indicates the method of construction best adapted to the inner box. The frames forming the sides and top would be of grille-like character, with vertical and horizontal bars considerably deeper than their thickness and close enough to enable a covering of parchment or any suitable material to safely withstand the external air pressure. Struts between opposite sides of the box, arranged in such a way as to interfere as little as possible with the operation of tuning, would, by balancing the external air pressure, permit the use of fairly light framework. An airtight door provides the necessary entrance. The outer box, preferably separated a small distance from the airtight box, would in a chamber organ be of ornamental construction, with venetians, controlled by a pedal in the ordinary manner wherever the design permitted.

An exhaust fan or some form of rotary exhauster, electrically driven and located as usual at a distance, draws air through an airshaft or trunk from the airtight box and obtains, and automatically maintains, the degree of exhaustion required. The best makes of rotary exhauster are self-regulating and can be relied on from zero to full power. But the ordinary bellows could be used to effect exhaustion if suitably valved and inverted.

The voicing of the pipes is not in any way affected, and all the ordinary resources of the organ builder are available with attenuated air as with air under pressure.

In the more complete chamber organs some stops of an imitative and solo character require a higher pressure of air than the others. I prefer to place such stops on wind chests supplied with compressed air, the resulting energy being that of the pressure and suction combined.

As but a small quantity of compressed air is required, it can be obtained from a small complete bellows, situated in or near the organ, and driven by an air engine operated by the exhaust system like the motor of automatic pianos, but of course larger.

This air pressure could be used for external stops such as an open diapason. The pipes, arranged to suit the design of the case, would then stand on independent wind chests and would be connected with the pneumatic action in the usual manner.

In effect, there would then be available three different wind pressures from two sources; one due to attenuation, one to compression, and one resulting from the combination.

In a like manner pipes could be supplied with air at a lower degree of attenuation, the regulator or reservoir being inverted. This reservoir, sprung or weighted to give the desired degree of attenuation, would be connected to a wind chest, on which the more delicate stops could be placed, and also, through the usual automatic cut-off valve, to the exhaust system. The difference between the attenuation of air in the wind chest and that of the air surrounding the pipes gives the effect of a reduced air pressure. This is only the ordinary practice under the reverse conditions.

The pneumatic action and controlling movements on attenuated air present no difficulty and need no description. All automatic pianos are so operated. They were used in the organ for a short time forty years ago, but were discarded because they involved an unnecessary wind system and an extra blower.

..... The elimination of the bellows and reservoirs enables the sounding board to be placed lower than usual near the floor, thus greatly increasing the height available for the pipes. Wind chests being unnecessary, the pallets can be seen from below, and the great disadvantage of the pallet to pipe system is removed. The air drawn into the box is of the surrounding temperature and dryness, and not, as in cases where the rotary blower is used to produce air pressure, supplied with air at a different temperature and, in wet weather, more or less moist. Discrepancies of pitch and the possibility of damage by damp are thus avoided. The hum or roar of the blower is not carried along the air shaft into the organ as it is with pressure systems, for the air is now drawn away from the organ. In echo and celestial organs, the airtight insulation of the pipes renders the illusion of distance more perfect, and for this reason they can now be incorporated with the main organ, when discrepancies of pitch resulting from differences of temperature, and the difficulties of a lagging response due to distance, are obviated.

Against these advantages there is of course a tonal loss, and the system described above is therefore limited to cases in which tonal output is of no great moment.

In a very interesting experimental organ built in Brentford by Mr. V. Willis and his sons, the author was especially surprised at the rapidity of articulation of the string toned stops in repeated chords. The many valuable features in that organ (both tonal and mechanical) should not be lost to the world now that organ building is resuming its former activity.

Sketches of Organ Mechanism
in Section.

THROUGH the courtesy of Messrs. J. W Walker, the author is able to present two drawings of a three manual organ containing octave and sub - octave couplers, both in tracker work and tubular pneumatics. The reader may profitably compare these with the laying out of the mechanism as shown in older books on the organ. Organists beginning their acquaintance with organ mechanism are advised to make a similar side sketch of any organ in which they may be specially interested, as it will be found most useful in remedying any faults that may arise, for it is not always an easy matter to trace such to their real source when there exists a considerable number of moving parts. The drawings will be easily understood if it is borne in mind that in tracker work the means of transmitting the key-impulse are as follows :—

1. The square, conveying the movements at right angles.

2. The backfall, which is simply a lever, and (as its name implies) the front part being pushed up, the back end falls. These are connected by pins working through them with either trackers, which pull, or stickers, which push.

In tracker work, the key resistance being considerable on pressures above 3in., much can be done to lighten the touch by means of "split" pallets. The pallet is partly divided in the middle, regulated by tapped wire and button so that the front edge begins to move first. The wind, rushing in, itself helps to neutralise the pressure from underneath and the result is a pleasant and elastic touch.

In pneumatic work, the touch can, and should be, so regulated as to resemble that of a good grand piano as to weight. Here, as explained in a previous section, motion may be transmitted either by the inflation of little motors or by their collapse. Builders have shown much ingenuity in their methods of using all these different means at their disposal, so that organs differing widely in their laying out require individual study.

Index to Contents.

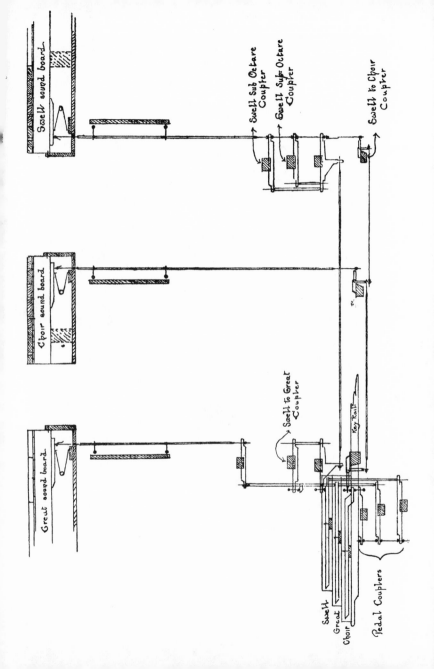

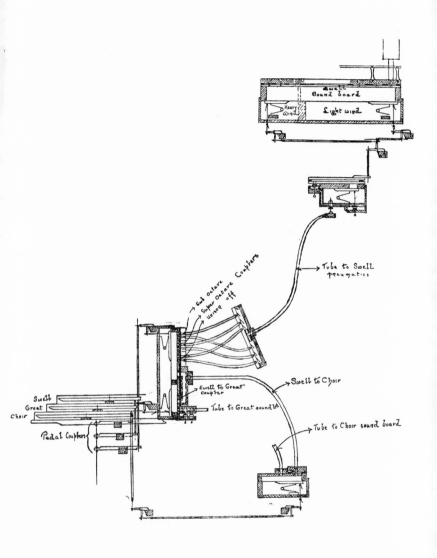